D0007270

THE CENTERS OF CIVILIZATION SERIES

LONDON
in the Age of Dickens

London

IN THE AGE OF DICKENS

By *Aldon D. Bell*

25659

UNIVERSITY OF OKLAHOMA PRESS
NORMAN

Library of Congress Catalog Card Number: 67-64446

Copyright 1967 by the University of Oklahoma Press, Publishing Division of the University. Composed and printed at Norman, Oklahoma, U.S.A., by the University of Oklahoma Press. First Edition.

To my father and grandfather
ALDON B. AND FRANK L. BELL

Acknowledgments

I HAVE HAD a deep affection for London since I first as a student visited the city fifteen years ago. During the many months I have visited or lived in London since then I find that the metropolis remains literally fascinating. After so much time I know only some parts of it and want to know others. I feel it is a never ending city, of which there is always one or more unique portions to know.

Curiosity about London led, for one thing, to this study of the city during a part of its many-layered history. I very much appreciate the opportunity which the University of Oklahoma Press has given me. As a consequence, I think I know just a bit better why this astonishing conglomeration of several millions of people which is called Greater London seems "comfortable" to me when most major Western European and American cities seem instead crystal hard, bleak, formidable, or frighteningly chaotic.

I want to state my appreciation to the General Research Fund at the University of Kansas, from which I was given a month and a half of scholarly leisure during the summer of 1965 to read more intensively about Dickens' London. Also, I owe much to my wife, Elisabeth Johnson Bell, for all sorts of help. To Malvern VanWyck Smith of Rhodes University, Grahamstown, Union of South Africa, I owe thanks as well. I have learned much, of course, from my faculty colleagues at the University (especially Professor Thomas R. Smith, chairman, Department of Geography), and from some superb scholars of Victorian studies who have in the past taught me: Asa Briggs, Francis H. Herrick, and Henry Pelling.

I have also learned a very great deal from the intelligent, interested, vigorous undergraduates whom I never cease to enjoy. They make academic efforts wholly worthwhile.

ALDON D. BELL

Lawrence, Kansas
June 1, 1967

Contents

LONDON
in the Age of Dickens

Approaches to Dickens' London

CHARLES DICKENS was born in 1812 and died in 1870. His lifetime spanned with near precision the greatest decades of English power and influence in world history. When he was twenty-five years of age, Victoria ascended the throne of the United Kingdom of England, Scotland, and Ireland. For thirty-three years he lived during the reign of Victoria. When he died, Victoria had thirty-one years of life remaining to her. A few of these years were as prosperous, as brilliant, and as untroubled internationally as those years of Dickens' maturity, but most of them fell into an era when Great Britain felt herself threatened in many crucial ways. Within a decade of Dickens' death, and actually somewhat earlier, Britain had entered an era of relative decline.

Dickens had not been born, nor did he die, in London. But no other famous Englishman of his time would be more associated with the life of the great metropolis. Dickens wrote all-encompassing novels which today give us a vivid taste of the size, condition, and character of London and Londoners: *Oliver Twist, Bleak House, Dombey and Son, Pickwick Papers*, and others. He did not intend them to do exactly that, and indeed they do far, far more. One of the greater thrills in recent years has been the rediscovery of Dickens—the realization that he was an artistic genius and not simply an entertainer.

3

But this is a book about London and not essentially about Dickens. His London was the greatest city in the world during his lifetime. Unchallenged, and given the historical conditions before 1914, unchallengeable, London cast a spell over foreigners and Englishmen alike. Its unquestioned diversity defied comprehension. The whole metropolis became a multiple capital. London encompassed the institutions of government of England, of the United Kingdom, and of the world-wide empire which was still growing. Great Britain's upper society, though still proud of "county" or provincial associations, made London its center. London served as the commercial, financial, and cultural capital of the empire. Whichever way one turns—save one, the world of new industries producing textiles, iron, heavy machinery—London was pre-eminent. In American terms, one had Dickens' London if one rolled Boston, Providence, New York, Philadelphia, Baltimore, and Washington into one relatively neat bundle roughly fourteen miles across from east to west and eleven miles across from south to north. Professor Asa Briggs called Manchester the shock city of the nineteenth century; anyone could identify and find distasteful what Manchester meant to, and did to, the people who lived there. London presented no simple façade, nor does she today. The casual American tourist (are there other sorts?) cannot "take in" London in three or four days; he can identify the superficial charm or other characteristics of continental cities. Consequently, he foolishly rejects London as unworthy of his time.

Englishmen of Dickens' era did not reject London; they simply could not take it in meaningfully, and consequently they accepted it as extraordinary. It did not fit any known patterns, new or old. It could not be managed. It had been

4

inherited from the eighteenth and previous centuries, and thus men must somehow just get used to it. More or less, they did. Or, as Ford Madox Ford wrote, London was incomprehensible by a single mind. London could be all things to all men; I would seriously doubt that such could be said of any other modern world city. In this sense, as well as in the sense which Neil Rasmussen used the phrase, London *is* "the unique city."

Every bit of knowledge that twentieth-century men learn about London's past enhances its importance in English history. Before the Roman conquest of Britain in A.D. 43, Britons had established a significant trading settlement roughly in the vicinity of London. Fully protected from the wildly rough Channel, yet easily accessible up the tidal Medway (the estuary of the Thames), ancient London sat where the Thames met the tides and where men had plotted several good fords across the river. During the century between Julius Caesar's abortive invasion and the actual Roman occupation Britons in London carried on a significant commerce with the Roman Empire. Under the Romans the settlement rapidly became an important center of the British province. "Londinium" assumed commercial, financial, and then administrative pre-eminence in Britain. It stored the major Roman military supplies and perhaps with Bath shared the distinction of being the only nontribal Roman center in Britain. Already London had asserted its cosmopolitan nature.

Historians once pictured crude Teutons wandering through the derelict streets of London after the Roman retreat from Britain in the fifth century. Again, the tiny pieces of knowledge, especially from archaeological research, indicate rather that changes were somewhat less dramatic. Certainly the Anglo-Saxon conquest and the wars between the Teutonic tribes and the Romanized Celts disrupted economic and political order in Britain. Yet London continued to be the most important trading center on the island. The Saxons shifted the physical center of London somewhat westward, and certainly London's influence reached less deeply into the remoter areas of the island, but commerce with the continent did not stop. In the sixth century the Christianizing of London was a crucial test for the new religion.

The movements of peoples emphasized the prize which they considered London to be. Alfred the Great sealed his salvation of Wessex from the Danish armies by the occupation of London in 886, after which event it became the center of English resistance. The life-and-death struggle of Wessex against the Danes now became an English reconquest of the island.

Between the death of Alfred in 899 and the death of Edward the Confessor (the last undisputed Anglo-Saxon monarch) in 1066 London's central importance in England became obvious to all. Trade and population increased, as did London's privileges granted by successive monarchs. Londoners already presented extensive and presumptuous claims: that, for instance, the "men of London" had the right to elect the kings of England. Although Anglo-Saxon and early Norman England had no designated capital, nor even the *concept* of a capital, kings, nobles, and merchants concentrated more and more of their significant activities in London or very nearby.

William the Bastard of Normandy fully earned his new title William I "the Conquerer" when he secured London after the Battle of Hastings. He built his greatest fortress

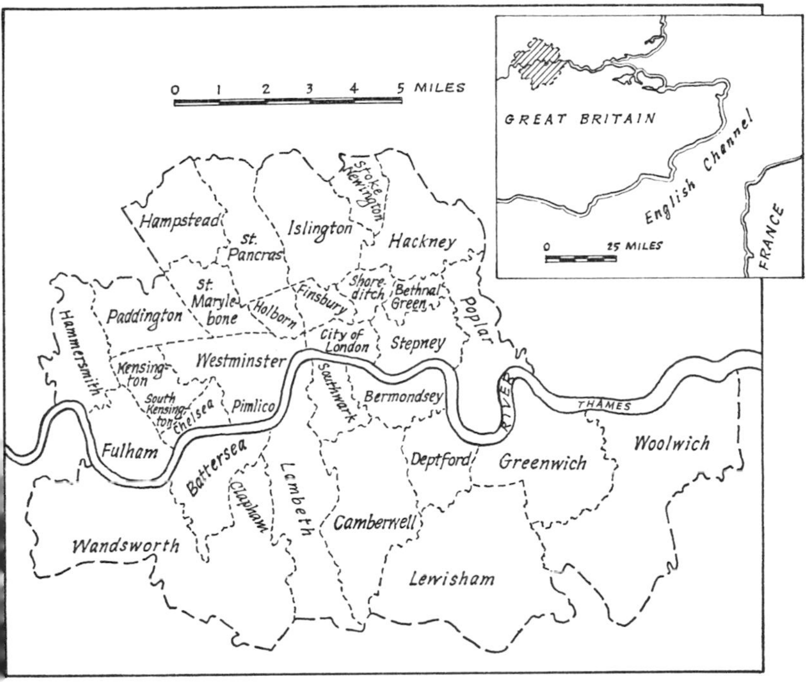

0 1 2 3 4 5 MILES
GREAT BRITAIN
English Channel
FRANCE
0 25 MILES
Hampstead
St. Pancras
Islington
Stoke Newington
Hackney
St. Marylebone
Holborn
Finsbury
Shoreditch
Bethnal Green
Poplar
Paddington
Hammersmith
City of London
Stepney
Kensington
Westminster
South Kensington
Chelsea
Pimlico
Southwark
Bermondsey
RIVER
THAMES
Fulham
Battersea
Clapham
Lambeth
Deptford
Greenwich
Woolwich
Camberwell
Wandsworth
Lewisham

MAJOR AREAS OF GREATER LONDON

just downriver from the City; the Tower of London protected, and awed, the burgesses of London. Henceforth, every monarch found London and her wealth useful, even crucial, to a successful reign. The Norman kings claimed Thorney Island (where Edward the Confessor had sponsored Westminster Abbey) as their own and built a palace there. With meticulous care and a continuing city pride, London bargained for more and more privileged security within the state. In national crises, such as the Wars of the Roses (1455–99) or the Civil War (1639–60), the support of London was vitally important to Edward IV, Henry VII, Oliver Cromwell, and Charles II.

By the eighteenth century London had fully consolidated that overwhelming pre-eminence within the kingdom. By the standards of the time, London's population was of almost terrifying proportions; it grew in spite of anyone's wishes and in spite of itself. One of the many faces of London frightened the aristocratic rulers of England: the London mob, an unknown beast, might turn on and destroy all rational order at any moment. With no standing army, no national police, no metropolitan-wide police, and no ready militia, the threat seemed real. The Gordon Riots of 1780 highlighted such fears; the Parisian mob after 1789 convinced any doubters. But London with its wealth, culture, society, politics, and sheer bulk defied solutions. England's elite learned to live with London, uncomfortably it is true, and not really understanding why it should exist as it did. They did not know what to do about it. In short, and to repeat, they got used to it. What happened in nineteenth century London is the subject of this book.

We have approached London in time like specially privileged travelers. Now let us approach it in space, historically.

A foreign traveler coming to London in 1870 would very probably have arrived first in Dover or Southampton and then journeyed by train to the metropolis. Such an approach would have been misleading and not at all enlightening except to the trained eye. The traveler approaching by water up the Medway would have had much the more accurate first impressions of what this fantastic metropolis was all about. Entering the Medway from the Channel at the Nore about sixty miles downriver from London, his ship (probably steam-powered, but with some sail) would have followed a well-marked, relatively well-dredged channel. To the right and left he could have seen marshes, flat fields, and poorly drained mud shores. The water would have become more contaminated with each mile; about forty-five miles up the Medway he would have seen, with some help, the very new sewer outlets and reservoirs spewing forth the wastes of more than three million people.

Still moving upriver, his ship would pass the Greenwich Marshes on the left and the outlet of Bow Creek on the right. London was near at hand, as probably the thin smog would have proved. Henceforth, the river's traffic increased rapidly, for the first of the great dock systems serving London would have appeared on the right. Small vessels would now be thickly mixed with the large seagoing ships. Veering sharply south to follow a great "U" of the river, the traveler would have seen more entrances to dock systems on his right, and then, ahead, at the bottom of the "U," the seventeenth- and eighteenth-century elegance of royal Greenwich. Then he would have seen more and more docks, with droves of small tenders and barges crowding around the cargo vessels.

After his ship had negotiated the "U" and turned straight

9

west upriver, the riverside slums of Stepney would have given way to more docks and more ships. Our traveler would have been entering "the Pool" of London, virtually an impassable conglomeration of ships, the life-center of the port. Nasty slums on the south bank and the famous Tower of London on the north bank announced the entry to the heart of ancient London itself.

Here, our traveler must move himself and his baggage to a lighter vessel, if he wants to stay on the river. Before moving under London Bridge, he would have seen the monumental Custom House and Billingsgate Market to his right, and more slums between massive warehouses to the left. St. Paul's Cathedral would have loomed through the inevitable haze to the right, and also Wren's Monument to the Great Fire of the seventeenth century.

After passing under Blackfriar's Bridge, he would have noticed a marked change. On his left he would have had still the dreary slums and warehouses, but to the north the other shore had recently been embanked. Immediately behind the Embankment he would have seen a series of famous sites: the Temple, Somerset House, in the distance the Nelson Monument in Trafalgar Square, St.-Martin's-in-the-Fields also on the Square. Then he would have turned south, under Waterloo Bridge, to see the magnificent Houses of Parliament (not yet a quarter century old) monumentally declaring the supremacy of British political institutions. He could, if he chose, move several miles farther up the Thames, past new housing developments, older Chelsea, and even more housing.

The river was the very spine of London. What the government, society, and even the railroads added to the flesh of the metropolis could not take away from the primacy of the Thames. Britain had her power on the sea. Her great naval bases were elsewhere on the outer coasts, but the jungle of shipmasts along several miles of the Thames represented the real nature of British strength. Britons had built this commercial strength in an earlier era, and now north-of-England industry added new dimensions to it. The almost unqualified optimism of 1870 would by 1880 give way to universal doubts, and doubts in turn give way to the reality of relative decline, but very few men expected serious economic trouble in 1870.

Dickens' Britain seemed unqualifiedly great; his London represented more aspects of this greatness than any other city in the Kingdom, or for that matter any readily identifiable geographical segment smaller than England itself. In a total sense, London was the "center of civilization" for nineteenth-century Britain: not the total civilization itself, by no means, but rather its historical, natural, and unchallenged center.

Briefly, we shall now look at the elements of London's greatness as Dickens knew it.

I

The English Century

◄▬▬▬▬▬►

WELLINGTON HELD, then routed, Napoleon's troops at Waterloo on July 18, 1815. Very nearly a decade earlier on October 21, 1805, Nelson beat the French fleet decisively at Trafalgar. Together, the two battles represented to Europe and an increasingly European-dominated world the essence of British power. Wellington had won victory with some 40,000 hard, disciplined, coldly effective British troops supported by 100,000 mercenaries hired to fill out the army. Grimly mauling wave after wave of French infantry and cavalry, the British-led army itself was ordered to attack decisively when Wellington knew Blucher and his Prussians to be ready-at-hand. British subsidies to a very considerable extent supported not only the nearby Prussians but the Austrians and the Russians coming up more slowly to give battle. British leadership, British discipline, British gold, some British troops, and continental allies: such were the components of victory. Nelson and the wholly British fleet had made Trafalgar another tale. Nelson's egomania cost him his life, but there off the Spanish coast the supreme confidence in men, ships, guns, and tactics assured the sanctity of the home islands and the supremacy of the British navy for decades to come.

The British people achieved their position of influence and power in the nineteenth century only after centuries of development. The story is, in fact, very largely one of English achievement, though associated peoples (Welsh, Scots, Irish, "colonials") contributed greatly. Since the humiliating defeat at the hands of France in the fifteenth century and the chaos of civil dynastic war (the Wars of the Roses) immediately following, England had found stability, prosperity, and continuity. The Tudors built up a central authority, the Crown, independent of papacy, continental powers, or major institutional restrictions domestically. Adventuresome Elizabethans picked at Spain, experimented in trade, and stumbled toward some understanding of national opportunities in an expanding European sphere. They found few answers to questions about government, social change, religious peace, justice, and liberty. Englishmen of the seventeenth century, ruled by Stuarts, Parliament, Oliver Cromwell, and then more Stuarts, rejected some possibilities of government, consequently indicating what they did *not* want. In the process they put down the foundation on which the politics of compromise could be built after 1689. At the same time in three wars (one under Cromwell and two under Charles II) England challenged successfully though not decisively the most powerful and enterprising commercial people of the seventeenth century, the Dutch. English seamen, pirates, merchants, explorers, diplomats, soldiers, and colonists claimed their place, minor though it might sometimes be, in the Americas, Africa, the Levant, and India.

Britain in the eighteenth century (Scotland and England united in 1707; Ireland remained a separate kingdom until 1801; Wales was a principality long since absorbed into England), ruled by a prosperous and self-possessed landed elite which also had a metropolitan base in London, fought throughout the world for trade and empire. Between 1689 and 1815, Britain remained the key power in five major wars or series of wars against France. Expanding agriculture, lucrative trade, and then basic industrialization supported the efforts which brought to the nation the prizes of Gibraltar, the West Indies, Canada, British Guiana, West African slaving stations, Capetown, Ceylon, large portions of India, and ports and stations throughout the world. And almost as impressively, Britain narrowly missed acquiring, for better or worse, Cuba, Buenos Aires, the Philippines, Java, and the Portuguese holdings in Africa. Even though a decided minority of the continental American colonists had successfully spoiled this record by rebelling in 1775, the total effort impressed all Europeans, not the least the British themselves. Trafalgar and Waterloo, Nelson and Wellington underscored and enhanced the previous work of a host of politicians, military officers, and merchants, including among the greater men Marlborough, Walpole, Chatham (Pitt), Clive, Shelburne, Hastings, and Pitt the Younger. With the defeat of Napoleonic France—indeed, in one sense, of Napoleonic Europe—Britain occupied the most exalted seat of power.

W. R. Inge, onetime dean of St. Paul's, wrote in 1953, at age ninety-three, that "the seventeenth and eighteenth centuries belonged to France, the nineteenth to us." In a real sense the years from 1815 to 1870 did indeed "belong" to Great Britain, but though she won pre-eminence and predominance, she did not have these in the sense of controlling ascendancy in European affairs. Supreme and apparently unchallengeable at sea, Britain needed on the continent of Europe allies or client states—or the utopian ideal of a Europe so intricately balanced among its states as to give Britain the opportunity to have its way by the mere threatening to join one or the other. What Britain wanted— the general principles and goals of her foreign policy— explains some of the intricacies of the British position in the nineteenth century:

1. To prevent one power from controlling the Atlantic coast of the continent and, in particular, the Channel coast.

2. To prevent one power or bloc of powers from winning overwhelming power in Europe.

3. To keep the seas open and safe for British commerce.

4. To win for British commerce at least equal privileges in the markets of the world, and to extend commercial privileges where feasible by diplomacy and the judicious use of force.

5. To defend the Empire.

Policy makers changed details but not the principles. Some writers have argued that from the 1820's George Canning established another great principle—that foreign policy should be responsive to public opinion. The statement is meaningless. Men of affairs had in the eighteenth century, too, made policy responsive to "public" opinion—that is, to the articulate, participating aristocrats who governed the nation. "Public" and "opinion" must be redefined constantly in this changing society of the 1800's. The middle classes and then the artisan working classes became part of the participating "public" by 1870. An extensive periodical press, an expanding newspaper press, and highly skilled pressure politics complicated the making of decisions. Some leaders even had to pay attention to the Catholic Irish in the nineteenth century.

In Britain of 1815 the fight against Revolutionary and Napoleonic France, the half century of nascent industrialization, and the antirational enthusiasm of the Evangelical Revival had not yet forced into submersion the eighteenth century. For fifteen years after the defeat of France, the British people exchanged ideas, insults, and occasional blows about the nature of their society. Not Britain, any more than France or the rest of continental Europe, was to be the same after what had happened in France in 1789 and thereafter. Most leaders from the traditional ruling classes recognized the inevitability of change. But what would be the extent of change, and at what pace? What institutions, what habits, what order of things could be saved, even enhanced?

The aristocratic leaders cautiously allowed the exuberant new forces and ideas to have their toe hold in the halls and drawing rooms of power, but the watchword was stability. Britain from 1815 to 1830 sought the balance between change and public order. The agents of order avoided excessive violence, prevented revolution, indulged in relatively little brutal repression, and, unintentionally for the most part, prepared the nation for more rapid change and improvement in later years. At this very beginning of the machine age they harnessed with considerable success the explosive energy of social, economic, and political change to the traditional though modified forms of British life. London, in particular, exhibited these compromises between old and new, between the proven and the unproven.

In these years of transition from indifferent eighteenth-century paternalism to enthusiastic nineteenth-century liberalism the complexities of British politics are intricate in their qualifications and confusions. In 1811, George III, never the tyrant or evil genius often portrayed, went hopelessly insane. The Regent, who became George IV on the death of his father in 1820, perfected his foppishness and foolishness until they became the symbols of a brief age. The best thing to be said for him was that he had, on occasion, good taste. Governing bored him; the enormous residual power of the Crown was, as a consequence, manipulated by the King's ministers responsible to Parliament. After George IV, a stupid William IV (1830–37) was succeeded by an eighteen-year-old girl, Victoria. By the time Prince Albert and Queen Victoria could again assume certain powers and prerogatives, beyond their symbolic functions, constitutional development had reduced their power to personal influence, which was nevertheless important on certain occasions.

Men of affairs used for political description after 1815 the terms "Whig" and "Tory," but both words had extremely restricted meanings. Whigs cherished the oligarchical traditions of the decades after 1689 and opposed the political groups dominant since 1783, when Pitt the Younger became prime minister. Tories, few of whom had any direct link with the Tory Party of the seventeenth and early eighteenth centuries, defended public order, continuity of administration (as long as that continuity was Pittite, as it had been since 1783), the Established Church—in general, the "Establishment"—against criticisms foreign and domestic.

In details Whigs and Tories differed enormously among themselves. The Whigs, a hopelessly declining minority, were dominated by the great oligarchical clans of the eighteenth century and were led, more or less, by Earl Grey. Grey opposed revolutionary activity and disorder, preferring the familiar forms of government; he pressed economy in government (especially in pensions and other spoils, since he was out of power) and favored the claims to full civil rights made by nonconformist Protestants and Roman Catholics. Grey, a casual politician who largely enjoyed his aristocratic prerogatives and fulfilled his class duty to his country, was a contrast to another self-styled Whig, Henry Brougham. Brougham boasted no great catalogue of acceptable connections and aggressively used forces outside politics (nonconformist, mercantile, and professional middle classes, and reformers of various sorts) to further his own ambitions. A brilliant lawyer with a superb mind and a talent for public campaign, Brougham disturbed Grey. Lord John Russell, the bumptious younger son of the Duke of Bedford, disturbed his leader less because of his impeccable Whig genealogy, but Russell also cultivated associations with some middle-class and nonconformist groups.

Also in opposition to the ministerial alignments were those harbingers of later decades, the Radicals. Counting for little in the House of Commons before 1830, they nevertheless argued the case for business interests, reform, the middle classes, and nonconformists. Alderman Wood of London, Joseph Hume (who added the catchword "retrenchment"—i.e., economy in government—to the old cry of "Peace and Reform"), and David Ricardo (though representing a rotten borough) competently but not brilliantly reminded England of alternatives other than traditional ones.

The government alignment of the decade and a half,

while even more diverse than Whiggery, gloried in talent. In fact, the Tories found almost too much competence and brilliance at their command. The "Ultra-Tories" on the right, the only true reactionaries in politics, admired the talent of Lord Eldon, lord chancellor with but one small break from 1801 to 1827. Eldon supported public order at all costs—indeed, to the extent of stirring up additional threats to his precious order by his judicial brutality. Slightly more moderate than Eldon, and perhaps better described as "high Tory," was the great hero of the day, Wellington himself: cynical, tough-minded, aloof, practical, and duty-bound. The Duke at moments of crisis transcended factional politics to insure administrative continuity. With Eldon and Wellington was Lord Castlereagh, whose mood was reactionary but whose reason forced him to counter the supremacy of reaction in post-Napoleonic Europe. The mental strain led him to suicide in 1822.

Three particularly brilliant younger men attracted attention. William Huskisson as president of the Board of Trade brought to the Tories new ideas about free trade, noninterference in the economy by the central authority, and fiscal soundness. Not personally popular, he still won valuable friendships with businessmen both in the City of London and in the new industrial towns of the north. Robert Peel, grandson of a yeoman farmer turned cotton entrepreneur, son of a cotton magnate who successfully bought his own and his son's ways into the traditional elite, was, like Huskisson, a first-class administrator. Peel even more deeply than Huskisson detested radical reform, preferring Pitt's technique of quiet, efficient administrative office and without noise, sought compromise between the change. Public campaigns disturbed public order; Peel, in old and the new. He governed Ireland as chief secretary from 1817 to 1822 in probably the most effective manner of any nineteenth- or twentieth-century official—though, of course, the miserable record of British government in Ireland makes any success seem a great one. Peel later turned his attention to penal and legal reform, again working quietly as home secretary while Brougham, Jeremy Bentham, and Bentham's Utilitarian followers campaigned publicly out of office.

Canning, Peel, Huskisson, Castlereagh, Eldon, Wellington—how could such a crew work together to adjust the nation and empire to the post-Napoleonic world? The answer to a very great extent was in one man, Lord Liverpool. Liverpool was apparently a dull, unimpressive, privately likable man. The son of a political fixer who won a peerage, Liverpool improved at the highest level on the talents of his father. He made the system he knew work; he had no other ideal. The 1820's resembled the whole of the eighteenth century in that the mere continuity of government was an ever-present problem. Men had not defined the constitutional relationships, nor built the political parties, which could provide continuity. Liverpool's ideal (in his own generation or in the generation of Lyndon B. Johnson) did not fire men's imaginations as did the words and principles of Canning, Brougham, or even Russell. The descent from this ideal to mere political fixing is quick, yet political and constitutional continuity is the most vital principle when a society is perilously near general confusion—not near to revolution perhaps, but to confusion due to social injustice, archaic political forms, religious intolerance, and moral irresponsibility. Liverpool kept young and old, reformer and reactionary, liberal and conservative, new man and landed aristocrat working more or less together. The government wrought important but tinkering sorts of changes and reforms. When Liverpool suffered a paralytic stroke, then death in 1827, the all-embracing Toryism of postwar adjustment came to pieces.

Domestic, foreign, and imperial policies all reflected the sorting out of old patterns under new pressures. Initially, stability had precedence over change, but gradually more change was acceptable. Liverpool's government gave the dominant landed elite the agricultural protection it demanded in 1815; the Corn Law made explicit the overwhelming interest of Britain's upper classes. Also, in the Currency Act of 1819 the government legislated an attempted return to the supposed financial stability before 1797. A complete return to payment in gold by 1821 restricted credit; here the government protected the fundholders, its creditors, even to the extent of damaging the landholding interests. The government thus gave strength to a major London interest, high finance. Along with these statutes, which pointed toward prewar stability, were the restrictive measures to crush agitation and disorder. Without a national police, the government used informers and stringent court judgments to dispel the last of the Luddite agitation in 1815–16. The Luddites, locally directed agitators and rioters against both agricultural and industrial exploitation of laborers, began their activities in 1811 and by 1816 blended into the more general discontent marking the postwar economic difficulties.

Radical societies disseminated the writings of Thomas Paine as well as pamphlets and broadsides. Simultaneously, William Cobbett, a nostalgic agrarian populist, growled his threats against London finance, while "Orator" Hunt with his artisan and shopkeeper crowds stirred all the major towns and cities. December, 1816, riots in Spa Fields and Clerkenwell in London confirmed the fears of the elite. Parliament suspended habeas corpus and legislated against the planning of "seditious" meetings. In Parliament's current mood any proposed demonstration was considered seditious. Protesting petitioners against the repression, the "Blanketeers," began a march from Manchester to London; Derby witnessed an outbreak. Both failed miserably. On August 16, 1819, the foolishness of authorities and troops caused the deaths of eleven persons on St. Peter's Field, Manchester. "Peterloo" (the radicals sneered an unforgettable comparison of St. Peter's Field and Waterloo) drew general protests even from some Whig aristocrats, but the ministry nevertheless asked for and got the very dubious Six Acts for further repression. Although radicals of all classes continued some meaningful agitation and demonstrations, many dissipated the energy of protest on the silly affair of Queen Caroline in 1820–21. The profligate Regent, now George IV, wished not to have the equally profligate Caroline crowned. She was not. Brougham failed to make political gain out of her cause, the King failed to get his divorce, and Caroline died in 1821.

With an easier economic situation after 1821, the radicals found fewer discontented Englishmen to agitate, and the government cautiously experimented with change. Huskisson freed trade, Peel studied reform in the Home Office, and Parliament repealed the Combination Acts against trade unions in 1824 (but renewed them in 1825, after an alarming outbreak of strikes). Commercial panic and depression struck the economy again in 1825. Agitators stirred up trouble for the government, and this time the simmering

Irish situation figured in the crises. Daniel O'Connell, one of those rare organizational geniuses in the history of Ireland who could bring virtually all the Irish into a campaign, had created the Catholic Association to demand political relief for Roman Catholics. With Liverpool's death the Tory ability to avoid major concession was lost. Canning governed England for six months before his sudden death; Lord Goderich kept a ministry more or less together for another five months until January, 1828. Then only Wellington could form a government, and it was a government which accepted the repeal of the Test and Corporation Acts against both Protestant dissenters and Roman Catholics. The "Protestant Constitution" of 1689 was dead; George IV died in June, 1830; the Wellington ministry, and the Tory supremacy which had lasted since 1783, also died by December, 1830. In 1830 the eighteenth-century aristocratic order was finally dispersed. Britain entered a quarter century of confident reform, change, and expansion.

In the Empire as at home, a desire to continue the old patterns, digest new acquisitions, and adjust to inevitable change marked the years 1815–30. By 1818, Britain through the East India Company had assumed control of all India to the Sutlej River in the northwest, the boundary of the Sikh state in the Punjab. No previous power in Indian history had achieved such unity; "India" had in fact been a geographical designation only. The British government supported the elimination of all other contestants for dominion in India but also imposed on the Company in 1813 the ending of its own trade monopoly with India. Both Company and Crown wished "consolidation" to be the theme in India, even before 1818, but consolidation sometimes led to expansion. Thus, Capetown, Mauritius, and a protectorate

over Zanzibar had been acquired to guarantee the sea route
to India, and in the 1820's the British took the first chunk of
Burma to stop Burmese piracy along India's eastern coast.
Elsewhere, Britain abolished the slave trade in 1807, thus
accepting a new humanitarian consciousness, but the navy
did little to enforce the ban until the 1830's. The central administrative structure in London, too inadequate to deal
effectively with such a vast empire, rarely troubled local
governors; Britain in fact had few reasons to pay very much
attention to the overseas dominions.

Europe, to some extent, taxed British ingenuity more than
either domestic or imperial affairs in these years. The som-
ber Castlereagh chose association with France and aloofness
from the wartime allies of Russia, Austria, and Prussia.
Stark reaction, whether holy or unholy, legislated against
British interest. Castlereagh more than any other man
wrote the congress system of great power consultation into
the Treaties of Paris, but at the Congresses of Aix-la-
Chapelle (1818), Troppau (1820), Laibach (1821), and
Verona (1822) he avoided continental involvement. Canning with more gusto and conviction continued after 1822
what Castlereagh had begun. Britain disliked the crushing
of Spanish constitutionalism by French troops in 1823 but
concerned herself more about the fate of the Spanish
colonies in America. Canning approached Monroe's administration about a joint declaration in support of independent
Spanish American republics, and consequently the Americans knew Britain's intentions and knew that Monroe could
safely pronounce his famous "doctrine." In 1824, Britain
recognized Argentina, Mexico, and Colombia, thus setting
precedence in a Tory era for the liberal dogma of "self-
determination." In the eastern Mediterranean the British

ran head on into a diplomatic dilemma: should they follow their sympathies and support the Christian Greeks in their struggle for independence from Turkey, or should they maintain the integrity of Turkey as a bulwark against Czarist Russia? In an enormously and, as we now see, perpetually complex situation, Britain with France managed for the moment to follow both policies successfully.

Historical periods are sometimes rather like seasons of weather. Men tacitly decide, either contemporaneously or in retrospect, what is normal and expected. Occasionally starkly abnormal variations attract everyone's attention, but also men sometimes sense a change when the annual facts and statistics do not support such a conclusion. Patterns have been changing for some time but have only just been noticed.

The history of Britain after 1830 is like this. Change, a new mood, and new attitudes rooted themselves in the past. Today we see no great watershed of human experience in 1830, yet the balance did shift. Many Britons thought the Reform Act of 1832 the end of a decent world, just as many thought it the belated beginning of one. It was, of course, neither. The peaceful extension of political rights to increasing numbers of people is one vitally important theme in nineteenth-century Britain, but there are others.

Overall, after 1830 the British people seemed to seize and relish the domestic opportunities and national power which had been won by 1815. Men of all classes met challenge more readily, hoping and working for better things. They made much of prosperity, personal freedom, private and public responsibilities. Proud among all classes of the British achievement, the nation not only asserted itself against other nations (or primitive peoples) to consolidate its position overseas. At home individual Britons also competed with each other as never before. Groups, more precisely organized, contested economic, political, and moral issues. Socio-economic classes, and especially the assortment of classes known as the "middle classes" because they were between the landed aristocracy and the unpropertied masses, aggressively demanded a full place in society.

Britain experienced a new mood; in substance, men held attitudes and opinions which were more varied than ever. If the aristocracy was "falling," the middle class "rising," and liberalism triumphant, one can find simultaneously the counterthemes and contradictions. In short, Britain had become an exuberant and restless nation, sometimes confident but often doubtful, experiencing before any other nation the excitement and pain of industrialization. Coziness was confined to the rural backwaters; the opportunities and the problems for mankind were vast and urban. Cities—large cities—channeled the new activity.

Men later called this combination of human experiences "Victorian," but it revealed itself resoundingly before Victoria came to the throne in 1837. Moreover, the British people experienced something quite different after 1880, when the Queen had yet another twenty-one years of life. Even by 1870, when Dickens died, a quiet caution and doubts about economics, religious faith, politics, morality, and British power crept into British awareness. From being a subtheme in 1830–80, doubt and uncertainty became the dominant theme by the decade of the 1880's.

We have seen that in 1830 George IV and the Tory ministry perished together. Indeed, the parliamentary elections constitutionally required after the death of a monarch went against Wellington's forces, and the Whigs came into office under the elderly, rather tired, conservative Earl Grey. Grey wanted one major change: the reform of the House of Commons. Such a reform involved an extension of the franchise to the less well-to-do, and a redistribution (i.e., reapportionment) of seats in the Commons. The crisis contained all elements to excite a nation: a die-hard but large Tory minority, penetrating and wide-ranging organized pressure groups, mass meetings in London and elsewhere, a sudden election in 1831, riots in Bristol, fears of revolution (France had had another one in 1830), a stupid and stubborn king, and a bitter House of Lords which finally had to be coerced politically. The Reform Act of 1832 eliminated the absurdities in the old constitution and did little more; however, public discontent had assured the passing of the act, and a precedent was set for future reforms. Britain still chose most of her leaders and politicians from traditional classes, but now an increasingly middle-class electorate had to be satisfied, placated, cajoled, bribed, or persuaded. The act changed slightly the tone of British politics.

New men did not dominate the new political scene after 1832. Brougham became lord chancellor in 1830, went to the House of Lords, and was thus isolated from mass politics. Russell, though always important, proved to be a moderate whose reforming image alienated Whigs and whose temper, ambition, unpredictability, and general ineffectiveness cut a peculiar and disturbing swath through politics. Middle-class radicals were loud in the parliaments of the 1830's and after, but they only very slowly increased their numbers from a few dozen.

Lord Melbourne, prime minister from 1834 to 1841 (except for a few months in late 1834 and 1835), infuriated the new men of the decade and has been badly mauled by historians. But was he the contradiction to the reforming mood that he seems? Like any eighteenth-century aristocrat (or twentieth-century undergraduate student), Melbourne pretended not to work. Men thought he dabbled at politics, thought administrative work a bore, preferred conversation and good company. He said as much. But a careful study of his career might instead prove that he often, even usually, worked very hard and was not lazy but deeply and secretly uncertain about constitutional and political relationships. Melbourne's frivolous manner might have been a personal mask for lack of decision, as was Russell's excitable temper or Gladstone's righteous indignation. Melbourne rode out one of the most tempestuous decades of the century; he had reason to wonder about the necessary decisions.

Parliament legislated several reforms after 1832. The Elizabethan Poor Law, elaborated on somewhat through the centuries, made way for the Poor Law of 1834. The new law reflected the assumptions and opinions of the rising industrial middle class, that the "poor" were largely vagrants, avoiding work and costing the taxpayers far too much money. Relief must be as unpleasant as possible, still offering subsistence. The working classes, especially in the cities and industrial areas, had pride and dignity which led them to hate bitterly the poorhouses established by the new law. The government could not enforce the law throughout the nation, Parliament (inspired inadvertently by fact-finding, "*laissez-faire*," economy-minded "liberalism") had given the working classes their greatest *cause célèbre* of the century.

In 1835, with more success, Parliament passed an act reforming (making uniform) the municipal corporations and

in 1837 began to modify some of the worst anomalies in the
Established Church. Parliamentary Radicals, more or less
representing the new ideas and new classes, attacked the
privileged classes, pensions, the State Church, the House of
Lords, government interference in the economy, the Corn
Laws, the army, the navy, the empire, and foreign policy.
For them, all represented the immoral burden of the present; as they functioned, they were feudal vestiges of a
medieval and antiquated order of things. In 1837, the most
vociferous Radicals established the Anti-Corn Law League
in Manchester and thus placed the starkly new of the industrial north in direct opposition to the amalgam of old
and new which was London. The League perfected the
techniques of mass persuasion and struck directly at the
defenses of the landowning peerage.

The working classes also threatened public order as it was
known. Reformers in 1830–32 had called workers into the
streets to help storm the aristocratic citadel. Robert Owen
and his followers in 1834 organized a multitude of local
unions into the Grand National Consolidated Trades Union; it collapsed in a few months. Melbourne's government
dealt viciously with rural discontent. Then in 1835 the
economy turned downward, and working-class discontent
looked to political reform. William Lovett and others established the London Working Men's Association in 1836;
the "Chartist" Movement had been launched. The People's
Charter included six demands: annual parliaments, universal
male suffrage, equal electoral districts, the secret ballot, payment for members of Parliament, and elimination of property qualifications for members of Parliament.

National in scope but not well organized, Chartism gave
vent to innumerable local, regional, and national grievances.

Chartists called the Convention in London in 1839, moved to Birmingham, and then had their great petition rejected by the Commons in July of the same year. The high tide of Chartism lapped at public order in 1839 before Melbourne left office, although Sir Robert Peel met a lesser climax in 1842 and Lord John Russell another in 1848. Middle-class politicians (Bronterre O'Brien and Feargus O'Connor, especially) tragically misled the Chartists, yet the workers, shopkeepers, and others in the movement learned permanently some hard lessons about social classes, political experience, organization, and purpose. Some talked about capitalism and the industrialists as bitterly as they had always talked of the landed peerage. The energy of Chartism was perhaps a negative reaction to industrialization and the problems of an industrial society; in the long run Chartism contributed much to the working out of ideologies for the positive control of an industrial economy.

Indeed, control of the new economic and social forces became an issue before Chartism. Already in 1833 Tory, Christian, and rural humanists expressed horror at factory conditions (working conditions, child labor, female labor, hours of labor). J. R. Stephens, Richard Oastler, Lord Ashley (later Lord Shaftesbury), and John Fielden (a high-handed factory-owning philanthropist) pressed Whigs and Tories for legislation. An inadequate Act of 1833 from the Whigs and an ineffective Act of 1844 from Peel's government finally led to meaningful legislation in 1847. Less precisely, literary figures such as Thomas Carlyle began to rail at the ugliness and immorality of urban industrial society.

Undoubtedly the most brilliant political figure of the period was Sir Robert Peel, also concerned about the new forces and the old order. Peel, always uncomfortable about the designation "Tory," preferred to call himself a "Pittite" (disciple of Pitt the Younger) or a "conservative." The Tories became the Conservative Party after 1835, though many within the party mistrusted Peel and the new designation. Peel held two principles above all others—indeed, one might call them assumptions: public order was a precious thing, to be preserved finally even to the extent of accepting a distasteful change; and (related to the first) continuity of government was the chief responsibility of all active politicians. Beyond these principles, Peel maintained preferences but no principles. He preferred the Established Church, the traditional elite, the paternalistic society, and an unreformed Parliament, but with dynamic changes molding a new society around him, Peel saw the need for adjustments to link the old and the new. This, presumably, he meant by "conservative." Many Tories considered such opinions betrayal of values and institutions worth defending at all costs, and they suspiciously watched their leader. The exhilaration of party victory in 1841 delayed the crisis, and Peel's ministry in retrospect seems a model for responsible cabinet government based upon a party with definable programs and principles. Actually, the talent of the men around Peel, Peel's own superb abilities, and the mediocrity of ministries after 1846 easily confuse us into seeing more constitutional foresight or party purpose than Peel had.

The ministry achieved much. Peel's own interest in a coherent administrative structure inspired the heads of departments at a time when bureaucratic elaboration was just beginning. The government further legislated the Church into the nineteenth century, set the official principles for banking and currency in the Act of 1844, and passed an inadequate statute on factory conditions. For drama and impact nothing, however, compared with the repeal of the Corn Laws in 1846. Peel had always favored little if any government intervention in the economy and sometime before 1845 apparently decided against the continuation of the protective tariff on grain. Irish famine and poor harvests in England decided the issue. Peel introduced the repeal measure and, in the greatest political (and socio-economic) crisis since 1832, carried the act with the help of Whigs, Radicals, and about one-third of his own party. The remaining Tories, now convinced that Peel was the most unprincipled man in public affairs, angrily attacked their leader. Peel probably could not have prepared the protectionist Tories for repeal, but he did not make the effort. For twenty-six years after 1846 the Conservative Party (it retained the name though Peel was gone) remained a minority in the Commons, slowy rebuilding itself under Lord Derby and Benjamin Disraeli.

After 1846, Britain entered a period of political confusion and economic prosperity. The revival of the economy in 1849 (and the humiliating failure of 1848) ended the Chartist agitation; most extraparliamentary pressures relaxed. In Parliament no single party or group could win a majority; all governments were in some sense coalitions (though only one officially so). Except for the Radicals, who tended to be industrial middle-class and therefore ardently demanded almost total acceptance of the new forces, each political group sought what it considered the vital center of public affairs. Russell wanted a reforming Whiggism willing to accept free trade and humanitarian legislation; Lord Palmerston, a more conservative Whig, sought a cautious balance with little reform, channeling the new energies into the Empire; the "Peelites" (Peel died after a riding accident in 1851) idealized Peel's effort but also saw the need for more change; the Conservatives inched toward acceptance of the new forces while preserving the outlines of aristocratic responsibility from the old order. These conflicts among groups, the resulting paralysis of the Commons, plus the obvious inadequacy of the state structure to deal with domestic and imperial affairs led virtually all politicians to the conclusion that reform of Parliament was again necessary. Each group of course sought to rearrange both voting requirements and seats in the Commons to suit its own purpose; every other group then must vote against such an attempt in order to defend its own position. From 1851 to 1861, the politicians tried reform, without success; they would not compromise, and an indifferent public did not force them to.

Out of the tangle, Lord Palmerston slowly won a personal popularity which smothered all other political considerations. The voting public appreciated his foreign policy and his national pride, and Palmerston wanted little or no change at home. Interestingly enough, Palmerston presided over the birth of the Liberal Party during his 1859–65 administration. All varieties of Whigs, Radicals, and Peelites acknowledged his popularity and joined his administration (partially in fear of a slowly reviving Conservative Party, which was the largest minority in a Parliament of minorities). Also, Palmerston reluctantly and skeptically accepted reforms and changes which individual cabinet ministers wanted; the Prime Minister did not impose his own ideas on the ministry. Thus Gladstone's budgets crowned the edifice of free trade, eliminating the last of the duties, tariffs, and bounties. Totally free trade had been a "liberal" goal since the 1820's; now it was a fact. By the time Palmerston died in 1865, newspapers regularly gave his coalition of groups the informal designation "liberal." The great Liberal Party thus came into existence, and Britain entered one of its rare periods of two-party government: Liberals vs. Conservatives, Gladstone vs. Disraeli.

Disraeli kept his place among the Conservatives in spite of the prejudice against him for his manners, literary ability, and Jewish origins. In 1868, he became prime minister after having as leader of the Commons in the minority Tory government guided the Reform Act of 1867 through the Commons. The Second Reform Act, more of a departure than the first, admitted the lower middle classes (shopkeepers, especially) and the artisans (skilled workers) to the franchise and granted new seats in the House to counties and large towns at the expense of small boroughs. This time the politicians could not dabble with the issue of parliamentary reform, for the working classes and many among the middle classes pressed a major agitation against all politicians. London, now more sophisticated and orderly than ever, witnessed a major portion of the agitation. The new trade unions (amalgamated societies with London offices, a central treasury, and a paid professional secretary) wanted a place in politics for the artisans because of unjust laws and the need for social reform; the middle class wanted prohibition, the ballot, destruction of the State Church, confirmation of free trade, economy in government, further rationalization of administration. The campaigns and agitation outside Parliament forced the politicians to make the necessary compromises, and the Reform Act of 1867 then brought to the constitution for the first time a mass electorate. Parties developed organization and coherence to meet the new challenges.

In the years after 1867 (or rather, after the election of 1868) a flood of legislation acknowledged the changes which Britain had experienced with industrialization. Gladstone's ministry from 1868 to 1874 disestablished the Protestant State Church in Ireland, fixed the outlines for universal (but not free) primary education, adopted the secret ballot, reformed the army (after the debacles of the Crimean War and the spectacle of German triumph on the Continent), rationalized the court system, stringently governed the licensing of pubs and liquor shops, and finished the opening up of Oxford and Cambridge to non-Anglicans. In many ways, nineteenth-century liberalism achieved its pinnacle of success in this ministry. Disraeli's government from 1874 to 1880 seemed to continue the process. Legislation dealt with the trade unions (more favorably than the Liberals), the sale of adulterated foods and drugs, slum housing, public health (sanitation), problems in agriculture, working conditions on merchant ships, primary education (now made compulsory), and more.

Yet Disraeli's legislation did more than simply extend social and economic reform; it emphasized a trend toward a stronger central authority and an extended administrative structure. Consequently, it reminds us abruptly of London, the nucleus of central authority. Administration had grown steadily since the Napoleonic Wars and most pronouncedly since the 1840's. Classic liberalism opposed central authority in favor of individual freedom, and while Gladstone's ministry destroyed or restricted privilege, Disraeli pressed reforms which stepped up the extension of administrative authority. Most of the Tory reforms required government inspectorates and new boards or commissions, but of course Tories had no basic, principled hostility to central authority. Disraeli's government thus reflected the centralization of the future as well as the hopes of earlier Victorians.

Britain lost economic buoyancy and optimism in the 1870's. Germany and the United States destroyed her industrial monopoly; the European depression spreading slowly after 1864 made businessmen cautious. The national mood after 1870 was, in fact, one of caution, consolidation, and protection.

Events in Britain of course affected the Empire, but imperial units, whether Crown colonies or self-governing colonies or "protectorates," followed courses somewhat their own. Britain increased her influence and control over the imperial units, but communications, domestic politics, economic considerations, and limited military resources always strictly limited the degree of control.

In the half century after 1830, India became one of the two vital poles of the Empire, the other being the United Kingdom herself. The British in India followed a certain logic of expansion which drew the subcontinent together under one authority. In 1839–42, Anglo-Indian authorities engaged in an adventure in Afghanistan. Russian intrigues in Persia and Afghanistan always sent a chill of fear through India and through officials in London; indeed, throughout the nineteenth century the British worried over the eastward expansion of the czars, the push south against Turkey, and possible Russian intervention in Central Europe. Indian officials, partly through genuine concern and partly through a desire to get more from a tight-pursed Parliament, saw Russian agents behind every problem save natural disasters. The Afghan adventure ended in disaster: British conquest, followed by a massacre of Anglo-Indian troops, followed by a punitive expedition to save British prestige.

But the failure here led India to conquer the Sind and then the Punjab; with the absorption of the latter (the Sikh state), no formidable independent state remained in the subcontinent. By 1848, the Punjab had been conquered.

Internally, the central authority (still under the Company) drew tighter the strings of Indian government. Especially under the Benthamite peer Lord Dalhousie, rational, "modern" ideas were pressed on the Indian substructure of authority. Dalhousie had no respect for the "illogical" Indian traditions and institutions, especially the Hindu. His administration as governor-general, added to the concerns of the traditional elite disturbed by Europeanization, contributed to the Mutiny of 1857. India did not experience a mass rising against British authority, nor was the mutiny planned and organized. The sepoys were joined especially by the Hindu elite, but loyal forces had won utter control by 1859. The previous year Parliament put an end to that peculiar governing institution, the East India Company; royal government came to India, and the Company became a commercial agent only. The central authority in India, now that of the viceroy, pushed relentlessly for centralization and coherence. The British created a nation of India when before the word was geographical only. Disraeli contributed further to the process when in 1876 his government gave to Victoria the title "Empress of India." Disraeli fully recognized the influence of the imperial past (Mogul) in India and the practical value of such a declaration in terms of the native peoples.

Around India, too, developed an Anglo-Indian empire in these decades. The conquest of Burma continued; a second adventure in Afghanistan failed like the first in 1876–78; in Malaya the scope of British "protection" expanded in the

1870's from Singapore (secured for Britain by Raffles in 1819). Calcutta, then New Delhi, governed or influenced deeply the largest portion of south Asia by the third quarter of the century. Indian as well as English trading interests led Britain to two wars with China: 1839–42 (when Hong Kong was taken) and 1856–60 (when the opening of China to the West was confirmed).

The home country, reluctant to support Anglo-Indian expansion, took more interest in securing the routes to the Asian empire. Before the 1860's the only sea route was, of course, around the Cape of Good Hope, where Britain had the magnificent harbor at Capetown. The Boers, never happy about British authority, increasingly threatened imperial security in southern Africa. After Parliament abolished slavery in the Empire in 1833, Boer discontent led to the "Great Trek" away from Capetown. In 1843, however, Britain declared Natal a British colony, preventing the creation of an independent Boer state on the coast northeast of the Cape. More aggressively, independent Boers also established settlements on the Orange River and beyond the Vaal River (Transvaal), but Britain seemed to obtain ultimate sovereignty over these settlements and at the same time to grant certain autonomy in the Conventions of Sand River (1852) and Bloemfontein (1854).

Events made the whole situation more complex, however. The Zulus threatened white settlements, and the wanderlust of the Boers irritated not only Zulus but other African peoples. Indeed, Boer atrocities against Kaffir peoples stirred the whole region. Cetewayo, who gradually after 1861 established himself as king of the Zulus, possessed skill in both governing and fighting; he became the most formidable threat to whites in all of Negro Africa. The

Zulu threat and gross misgovernment of the Transvaal led Britain to annex that settlement in 1877; British soldiers and British money then had to be expended in a war against the Zulus in 1878–79. The Boers in the Transvaal did not appreciate being saved from the Zulus and only marked time until they could win total independence from Britain. Independence, made more feasible by the discovery of gold in 1871, threatened imperial interests—not because of the gold but because Germany or France might interfere in an area near the precious route to India. But now we anticipate the Anglo-Boer conflict after 1880, which led to war at the end of the century.

In northern Africa the Empire necessarily found itself deeply involved by the 1870's, for French entrepreneurs in 1869 opened the long-dreamed-of Suez Canal. Britain now witnessed the opening of a second route to Asia, more expensive than the route around the Cape, much shorter and faster, and exceedingly vulnerable to powers bordering on the Mediterranean. Disraeli purchased seven-sixteenths of the shares in the Canal in 1875, involved Britain with France in the Egyptian debt commission, and acquired Cyprus from Turkey as an eastern base. Gladstone reluctantly and ironically occupied Egypt after 1880, leading Britain to greater and greater expansion to protect the routes to India.

Canadian events moved the Anglo-Saxon colonies toward new relationships with Britain. The complex Canadian Rebellion of 1837 (actually two, and perhaps three, separate rebellions), and the Canada Act of 1840 (establishing "responsive" self-government) allowed Governor-General Lord Elgin to establish responsible parliamentary government on the British pattern. The British North America Act of 1867 recognized and defined what we today would

call "dominion" status; the Empire moved nearer to being
the Empire-Commonwealth. In Australia the various colonies convinced Britain finally to end all penal transportation by 1868; the development of wool-producing after
1830 and the discovery of gold in 1850 boosted the continent's importance. New Zealand by 1870 had won peace
with the Maoris and responsible government from Britain.

The expanding, consolidated Empire complicated Britain's relationships with major world powers, but shifting
power balances in Europe did the same. From 1830 until his
death in 1865, Palmerston virtually personified his nation's
foreign policy. In general, Palmerston the Whig followed
the general principles of policy defined by Castlereagh the
high Tory and Canning the radical Tory. More than Canning, perhaps, Palmerston in the exuberant days of liberalism and continental revolution encouraged constitutional
government and middle-class revolutions; certainly Palmerston had more opportunities to judge revolutionary movements in Europe.

In the first two decades of Palmerston's dominance of the
foreign office (though he himself was out of office from
1841 to 1846), Britain's rivalry with France intensified certain problems. The two nations worked uncomfortably together against the eastern powers; competitive interests in
Belgium, the Iberian Peninsula, and the Eastern Mediterranean (again!) led to difficulties. When Palmerston came
to the foreign office in 1830, the Belgian revolution greeted
him. He sympathized with the Belgian cause against the
Dutch but feared French dominance of a new Belgium—or
even French annexation. That stretch of Channel coast must
not fall to France. The London Conference of 1830–31 led

to a settlement the following year; an Anglo-French intervention forced the settlement on the Dutch. Later Palmerston won from all the great powers neutralization and defined frontiers.

Civil war in both Spain and Portugal complicated British interests, but in both countries the British supported winners (so much as any side can be said to have "won," especially in Spain). A jealous France under Louis Phillippe intrigued to obtain marriage alliances in Spain, won them in 1846, and utterly destroyed any immediate possibility of further Anglo-French co-operation. In the eastern Mediterranean the English, however, had already dealt abruptly with the French. France and England had co-operated to contain Mehemet Ali in Egypt and along the Levantine coast, thus preventing him from weakening the whole Turkish Empire. But France, which had what it considered residual interests in Egypt and along the Levantine coast, began through Thiers (prime minister in 1840) to hope for Mehemet Ali's success. Palmerston simply arranged an eastern settlement with all the great powers except France, humiliating her; in 1841, the powers signed an international treaty closing the Dardanelles to warships if Turkey were not at war.

Palmerston's highhandedness and supreme confidence in his own judgment revealed themselves most forcefully from 1848. He gave all the support he could to liberal revolutions throughout Europe. Victoria and Albert distrusted him and complained that he did not keep them informed. In 1850, he dealt abruptly with Greece over the very dubious "Don Pacifico," who had some claim to British citizenship. In trouble with Parliament, Palmerston then eloquently pleaded the cause of British rights throughout the world. When he indiscreetly expressed approval of Louis Napoleon's *coup d'état* in France, however, he was forced to resign.

Not Palmerston but a weak coalition ministry allowed Britain to fight a useless war with Russia in 1854–56. The "Crimean War," as it was called, released some of British paranoid fear of Russia and proved the gross inadequacy of the British army and all its services. British support to Italian unity signified more in European affairs. And most important of all were the rapid changes in Central Europe which totally readjusted the whole European balance. British statesmen had long misjudged the various German states but seldom had they so miscalculated affairs as in the 1860's. They necessarily watched America closely and followed an extremely cautious policy during the Civil War; but Russell and Palmerston and Gladstone and hosts of lesser officials need not have spent all their judgment elsewhere. Britain totally missed the significance of the Austro-Prussian War against Denmark in 1864; she thought Prussia had no chance whatsoever of outmanuevering Austria in Germany. The Austro-Prussian War in 1866 astonished the British, for they grossly underrated Prussia's army. Finally, the Prussian conquest of France in 1870–71 and the declaration of the German Empire dramatically illustrated the new balance with which Britain must contend. Disraeli's (he was now Lord Beaconsfield) brilliant diplomatic games of 1875–79, when a new Balkan and Russo-Turkish crisis involved British interests, simply obscured the fact that other problems loomed for Britain and her Empire. Bismarck, after all, not an Englishman nor a Frenchman, presided in Berlin over the great conference of powers which tried to sort out the Balkan mess.

By the decade of the 1870's, events had radically qualified Britain's dominance. It was no longer an "English century." France and Germany would soon challenge British naval supremacy; all major powers could intrigue against or directly threaten portions of the Empire or the routes to India; situations in Africa, Asia, the Pacific, and Europe demanded extensive and even extravagant use of British resources. Britain had already entered an age of "relative" decline, for her previous weaknesses were more obvious than ever, her new ones could not be obscured, and her previous strengths were less important.

London, as a capital city in as total a sense as is perhaps possible in major nations, observed these public affairs, witnessed the formulation of decisions, and communicated both the decisions and impulses of British society to a large portion of the world. The rich, relatively comfortable metropolis channeled so very many of the life-forces of the nation, and these forces in turn manifested themselves in the historical facts of power, influence, and expansion.

From Dickens' London one could view the world.

II

The World Town

LONDON in the nineteenth century became the greatest urban center in the world—the "world town," Ford Madox Ford called it—capping its steady, persistent growth of centuries. Roman London already held about 45,000 people; Elizabeth's probably had not quite reached 100,000. By the time George III came to the throne in 1760, the metropolis had passed 750,000. In 1801, the year of the first official census, that area which in 1889 became London County held 865,000. When Dickens died in 1870, there were 3,250,000 inhabitants, and adjacent areas in Middlesex, Surrey, Kent, and Essex were being drastically changed by London's growth. The prosperous middle class had built "suburbia," though not yet could it be said as it can today that in effect all of southeastern England was "London's region."

Greater London (now the City of London, City of Westminster, and twenty-eight boroughs) had two potent nucleuses from which to develop. The City of London to the east ("the City") featured the port, warehouses, industry, and finance; Westminster to the west possessed the Court, national government, and town houses of the aristocracy. The Strand connected the two, both of which had long since begun to spill over in all directions. The slums which housed the workers in the City and on the docks attached themselves to the City. Beyond the slums, the middle classes built their modest, dull sections within relatively easy reach of the City. The outer ring of Westminster housed more of the middle classes, with some working classes. Forming the crudest kind of mosaic, the railroad finally gave the segments some unity and allowed the surge outward into the suburbs.

Most observers or travelers visiting an urban center for the first time view it as a glob of humanity, differing from the previous glob only in size. The picturesqueness of countryside is more immediately comprehensible; the diversity of a metropolis takes careful observation and understanding.

London especially defies the visitor, unless some effort is made to recognize the many segments. Ford would have disagreed with this statement, for he wrote that a single mind could not possibly comprehend London. He had only two categories of thoughts regarding London; those which dealt with the whole mass, and those which dealt with the atomized individual human beings who lived there. He ignored the complexity of districts within the metropolis, where human associations and characteristics differed radically from those in other districts. If we glance at least briefly at the major segments, beginning in the east and on the north bank of the river where London began, then moving very roughly counterclockwise until we are again in the east and on the south bank of the river, then at least we can identify the major distinctions within the mass.

To the east, beyond the boundaries of the City of London, the economic activities of the City had already laid the foundations of the "East End." Stepney with its great accumulation of warehouses, docks, industry, and working-

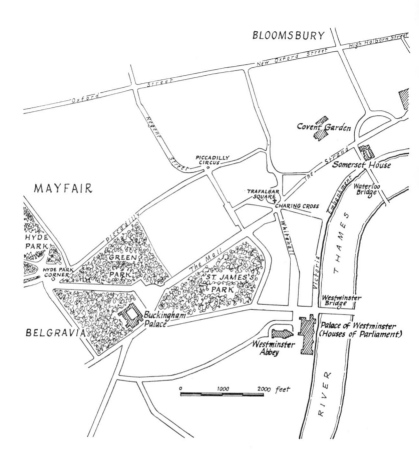

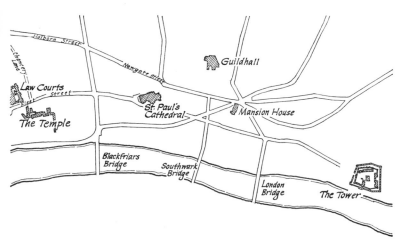

Holborn Street

Chancery Lane

Newgate Street

Guildhall

Law Courts
Fleet Street

St. Paul's
Cathedral

Mansion House

The Temple

Blackfriars
Bridge

Southwark
Bridge

London
Bridge

The Tower

CITY OF LONDON AND WESTMINSTER: MAJOR LANDMARKS

47

class quarters was the very heart of the development. By mid-century, Stepney had a quarter of a million people, no public drainage at all, and a reputation for vicious cholera epidemics. Indeed, cholera arrived in the kingdom from the Eastern Mediterranean, and usually through the London docks on merchant ships from Turkey, the Levantine coast, or Egypt.

Immediately to the north of Stepney lay Bethnal Green, the site of the most infamous nineteenth-century London slums. Farther east still, beyond Bethnal Green and Stepney, the great expanse which is now the borough of Poplar experienced virtually a boom development during the wars against Napoleonic France. The north basin of the West India Docks, the East India Docks, and major roads to the City encouraged rapid economic expansion. Poplar was divided from Stepney in 1817 and made a separate parish. Proximity to the great river had governed this initial economic development, but new roads and railways connecting Poplar with the City changed all this by mid-nineteenth century. Economic development no longer relied utterly upon waterways. Hackney, a vast manor north of Bethnal Green, Stepney, and Poplar, had been semirural when George III died in 1820; in the decade of the 1840's half the area still was marsh or grass. After 1850 the East End literally absorbed Hackney. The working classes had a new suburb.

Shoreditch, immediately to the north of the boundary of the City, had become a part of urban London in the eighteenth century. By 1850 social snobbery, the growing but chaotic furniture industry, and timber business needing a good deal of space caused the monied families to move out. A decade later the 100,000 inhabitants of Shoreditch (largely working class) lost ground to the great office complexes, warehouses, and workshops spilling over from the City. North of Shoreditch the village of Stoke Newington, an earlier Quaker center, filled in slowly from the south. And finally, as far as developed area most directly related to the City is concerned, Finsbury (also north of the City, and west of Shoreditch) saw before 1840 the building of pleasantly planned and often tastefully built middle-class residential areas. Here in the 1700's had lived nonconformists wishing to evade as much Establishment supervision as possible, and now in the nineteenth century the office clerks, lesser merchants, and professionals (the second rank in the troops carrying forward the vast economic conquests of nineteenth-century Britain) occupied northern Finsbury. The south of Finsbury adjacent to the City became commercial with offices, factories, and warehouses.

Not so directly related to the City was the great pie-wedge of development beginning north of the Strand. Grim slums in the Aldwych area became grimmer still at St. Giles', which until Shaftesbury Avenue was cut through contested with Bethnal Green's as the best known slums of the metropolis. Here in the miserable Holborn slums, falling between the two stools of City and Westminster, the infant death rate was probably the highest in all of Britain. Beyond the slums to the north of Holborn the Duke of Bedford had begun in the eighteenth century to build the still exciting pattern of residential squares which became "Bloomsbury." The squares, such as Bedford Square and Russell Square, provided cells of well-to-do residences, between which provisions shops and artisan services grew up. By 1800, Bloomsbury was flowing north in less well-to-do terraces of houses, and the builders kept up the momentum into southern Islington (again an earlier nonconformist center beyond the immediate jurisdiction of the City or Westminster). Northern Islington remained rural until after mid-century.

The great, sprawling area of St. Pancras (north and a bit west of Holborn) had disconnected segments of population until the builders got hold of it in the early nineteenth century. After that, the railways came. The lines slashed their way north from Euston Station (1836), King's Cross (1851), and St. Pancras (1868). Though plastered over with building, the railways dissected St. Pancras more than before, ruining great chunks and long stretches in the process. With exception of fashionable Highgate, slums filled in the parts of St. Pancras which survived between railway stations, rail lines, and major roads.

Moving west again, the wedges of development related themselves to Westminster, not to the City. Some of the Prince Regent's grandiose ideas, magnificently planned and executed by Nash, found expression in Regent Street and Regent's Park. The great villas in the park (twenty-six originally planned, only eight built) and the terraces of fine houses around the park encouraged the growth of St. Marylebone, which was otherwise entirely built over with middle-class housing by 1850. As this development scratched its dull way north, it met Hampstead coming south. Hampstead on its Heath had been fashionable and arty for some time. Now the charm of eighteenth-century and early nineteenth-century Hampstead, together with the early stucco and later brick bourgeois homes, became part of London. No open area separated Hampstead from the metropolis.

Paddington, still village-like in 1820 and still with Tyburn

Gallows until 1825, provided room for some quite fashionable residential development north of Hyde Park. The Bishops of London owned Bayswater lands, and there "Tyburnia," a relatively attractive early nineteenth-century development, grew up. The lower middle class soon followed the more fashionable inhabitants, filling in the gaps of land with stuccoed villas. At mid-century the railway arrived—not, however, bringing with it quite the same havoc that it brought to St. Pancras. Paddington Station with its lavish hotel was begun in 1850. Some areas nearby declined to slums afterward, but the more sordid and neglected housing areas filled the far northwest corner of the borough. West of Paddington the borough of Hammersmith (part of Fulham until 1834) possessed large stretches of open space until the 1860's, after which period the whole area became one great middle-class suburb.

Having come half circle from the East End around the north and now back to the river on the west, London's expansion presents yet another aspect. Again the Prince Regent influenced events. His decision to make Buckingham House, owned by royalty since 1762, the official London residence of the monarch naturally encouraged fashionable building nearby. The Grosvenors (now Dukes of Westminster) commissioned Thomas Cubitt to develop "Belgravia" to the west of the Palace. Cubitt started building his streets and houses in 1826, and the end result was a supremely fashionable aristocratic quarter. As always, the less fashionable followed the so-called great. Pimlico, from having been market gardens supplying Westminster customers up to the 1830's, was built over as an outer ring of Belgravia. The elite and not-so-elite moving still farther south and southwest of Belgravia reached Chelsea village after mid-century, which as an outlying retreat for aristocrats had enough charm and quaintness to appeal to artistic folk who wanted to be part of, but not in the very midst of, the metropolis. Kensington, to the west of Kensington Gardens and consequently to the north of the Belgravia-Pimlico-Chelsea development, began its development in the 1830's and 1840's and then after mid-century became an educational and institutional quarter. Finally, London absorbed Fulham later in the nineteenth century, where until 1850 lush market gardens near the river helped to supply the metropolitan market.

London's growth north of the Thames impressed everyone, but the history of South Thames is that of a fantastic boom. From Roman times until the eighteenth century one crossing, London Bridge, led to the south. The building of Westminster Bridge (1750) and Blackfriars Bridge (1769) guaranteed new interest in the more accessible region. Within four years of the Battle of Waterloo three new bridges—Vauxhall in 1816, Waterloo in 1817, and Southwark in 1819—further opened up the south bank. The City completed new London Bridge in 1831. With six river crossings and the beginning of the railroad era, South London changed as rapidly as any area in the kingdom.

Southwark ("the Borough") had an ancient development as the southern approach to London Bridge; by 1850, vast warehouses and intervening slums characterized it. Following downriver to the east, the Surrey Commercial Dock Company chose Bermondsey for its docks which it began to build in 1809. Warehouses and slums followed the docks. In fact, the shockingly miserable condition of working-class housing in Bermondsey led to early rebuilding and experimenting with model dwellings. Deptford, east of

Bermondsey, had slums, warehouses, and factories along the river, and middle-class suburbs to the south away from the Thames.

Beyond Deptford the pattern changed. Greenwich, because of the royal establishments (Greenwich Palace, with Royal Naval Hospital) and because of picturesque Blackheath, had been popular with the aristocracy and plutocracy for two centuries. Nineteenth-century development did not engulf the earlier parts, even though the "gentle folk" left after 1830. London actually absorbed Greenwich only around mid-century and did not take in Woolwich until the late 1800's. Woolwich with its Royal Arsenal, Dockyard (until 1869), Royal Military Academy, Royal Artillery Barracks, and notorious working-class slums had grown westward toward London, especially during and after the Crimean War (1854–56). Upriver or west from Southwark, the spreading metropolis left the market gardens of Battersea inviolate until the 1840's, but the railways offering quick access to the north bank changed that situation. Battersea and Lambeth both became stretches of middle class villas.

South of the riverside boroughs the *bourgeoisie* soon filled all available open space with their sameness and took over what had been fashionable. Wandsworth on the west filled in between 1820 and 1870. It included Clapham, which had been another of those separate villages close enough to London to be ripe for fashionable occupancy in the eighteenth century. Clapham gave its name to "the Saints," the Clapham Sect, those wealthy evangelical Anglicans who poured low-church morality into politics, sometimes with good results (as in the abolition of the slave trade in 1807). Camberwell, immediately south of Southwark, filled in its fields with middle-class housing by the 1870's. And finally, Lewisham in the southeast had just begun to build by 1870.

We have come full circle within which lived the three and a quarter million Londoners in 1870. How, then, did so many people make a living?

London from the Roman beginnings meant, before all else, the river port. The court of the English kings settled itself at Westminster to be near London, but not in it, for the merchants of the City were among the chief financial assets of the kingdom. With increased enterprise overseas, as the British seized markets from the Spanish, Dutch, and French, and native peoples, stable financial institutions and successful commercial practices attracted capital and capitalists from Europe. The port, finance, and the massed population encouraged industry, first of the craft sort and then mechanized. Directly or indirectly, then, the whole complex structure of Victorian (and later) London supported itself on the port, established on that splendid site on the upper reaches of a tidal estuary.

The British economy in the early eighteenth century became decidedly commercial as well as agricultural, and after 1760 or thereabouts industrialization added yet another facet of growth. Except when Napoleon's decrees or Britain's own orders-in-council restricted British commerce, the increase encouraged new and steady development of London's port. From 1799, businessmen formed companies to build the great docks needed for the increased traffic. In that year the West India Dock Company began the docks of that name in Stepney, off Limehouse Reach; in 1802, they were open for business. In 1805, another company built the London Docks almost two miles nearer to the

City; the promoters eagerly pointed out the advantage of being so near the great commercial center.

Before the Battle of Waterloo, two other docks were built. The East India Dock in the Poplar section of Stepney, and northeast of the West India promotion, catered to vessels of the East India Company. The rapidly expanding India and China trade encouraged the scheme. On the south bank in Bermondsey, yet another group built the Commercial Docks, at which timber and wood products became the primary business. No further development came for two decades. In 1829, a company opened the St. Katharine Docks. The new docks, enormously expensive because they displaced 6,000 inhabitants, more than 1,100 houses, the Royal Hospital, and the Collegiate Church of St. Katharine, had two vital assets: proximity to the City (immediately adjacent to the boundary, which actually ran between the City and the London Docks), and enormous warehouses for the use of clients. The incredible warehouses of the London and St. Katharine dock system (the companies amalgamated in 1864) still stand and have since the early nineteenth century provided the specialized handling necessary for many classes of imports.

The next dock work was promoted at mid-century, largely because of the increased size of ships. In 1855, the Victoria Dock (now the Royal Victoria Dock) provided deep, spacious facilities with the first mainline railway connection of any London dock. Far to the east, beyond all other docks and actually across the river from Woolwich, the Victoria Docks became the basic unit for the Royal Albert (1880) and King George V Docks (1910). The "Royal" Docks attracted the bulk imports: grain, foodstuffs, tobacco.

Economic realities forced the rationalization of this enormously important but disconnected private enterprise. In 1838, the East India and West India Dock Companies combined to form a new company, and the London, St. Katharine, and Victoria Companies followed that example in 1864. Not until 1909, however, did the national government create the Port of London Authority to include all docks on the river.

The national government early in the nineteenth century forced other improvements upon the chaotic management of the Thames as a commercial roadway. Six centuries earlier in 1197 the Crown had given to the Corporation of the City of London the privileges and obligations of keeping the Thames open for traffic. In fact, the City took little or no responsibility for the stretches below the City itself, doing only what was absolutely necessary to keep a channel dredged and open. Businessmen and politicians bitterly criticized the indifference, incompetence, and failure of the City, and in 1857 Parliament finally authorized the creation of the Thames Conservancy.

All of these improvements (docks, conservancy, warehouses, railways) involved the Pool of London and stretches of the Thames largely downriver, but more of the metropolis needed waterway attention. Old London Bridge had restricted the tides above it, but after 1832 when the last of its piers were gone the increased tide upriver made navigation dangerously irregular. Economic depression, dock development, and war delayed action, but then in the 1850's the concern for sewage disposal drew another sort of public attention to the riverbanks above the City. In 1863, Parliament provided for embankments above London Bridge to help regulate the river, to eliminate the large stretches of stinking mudbanks at low tide, and to serve as sites for sewer outlets. Engineers and workmen finished the impressive jobs in the five years from 1869 to 1874. The Albert Embankment reached on south bank from Lambeth Bridge, virtually on the doorstep of the Archbishop of Canterbury's Lambeth Palace, to Vauxhall Bridge just over half a mile upstream. Londoners and visitors know best the Victoria Embankment running from the north end of Westminster Bridge all the way downriver to Blackfriars Bridge in the City. Sir Joseph Bazalgette who engineered the embankment created the most pleasant river walk and river drive in modern London as well as a functional master-piece. Finally, the Chelsea Embankment on north bank was finished in 1874.

Other engineering works of the nineteenth century made the port even more important. In 1801, a promoting company planned the Grand Surrey Canal to bring fresh produce from Epsom, Croydon, and Camberwell to the Thames at Bermondsey. The canal, construction for which started on the river, did not get beyond Camberwell, but it has served magnificently to feed bulk cargo to the great Commercial Docks. To the north, too, a great canal was planned and built in 1812–20. The Regent's Canal connected the Grand Junction Canal terminus in Paddington with the Thames at Limehouse. The canal ran along the north edge of what was then built-up London: Regent's Park, St. Pancras, Islington, Shoreditch, Bethnal Green, and south through Stepney. The railways, of course, provided increasingly important feeder lines for the port from the 1830's on.

The development of the bonded warehouse system after 1803 allowed London to offer importers and exporters especially convenient facilities, and the Crown also finished in 1817 the vast Customs House upriver from the Tower. Customs officers dealt more rapidly with goods afterward, but not so rapidly as after 1861, when Great Britain enjoyed totally free trade. The government reduced or abolished tariffs, duties, and charges from the 1820's to the 1860's, until none at all remained. Protective tariffs in the twentieth century, however, put the Customs House back into use.

Whether protection for an ancient trade, or free-trade hatred for a central monopoly, the preservation of watermen's rights proved a boon to one portion of London's port. The watermen (most of whom lived in Stepney) had unloaded the cargo ships on the river before the great development of docks, and all parliamentary authorizations for dock companies had guaranteed the free access to docks of any carriers. This "free water" clause meant that ships could unload at the docks, and then the wharfingers could with barges or other small carriers take lighter cargoes upriver. The guarantee thus unexpectedly allowed not only increased warehouses and specialized storage facilities to be built where no large docks served them, but also industrial plants needing port access in order to develop could be established upstream. Industry using smaller water carriers could grow up everywhere with access to water routes leading to the docks.

Regarding this activity, a list of exports from London's port in the late 1860's in order of value illustrates the nature of the metropolitan economy:

1. Textiles and all related products, including ready-made clothing (cotton, wool, silk, and linen, in that order).

2. Iron products.
3. Copper products.
4. Leather and leather products.
5. Machinery.
6. Beer and ale.
7. Hardware and cutlery.
8. Other metal products.
9. Earthenware and glass.
10. Firearms and gunpowder.

The ships entering London's port brought an enormous variety of food products, raw materials, and manufactured goods in that order.

Concerning the ships and tonnage, almost exactly half of all water-borne tonnage entering London in the 1860's was coastal; fifteen per cent was from the empire; thirty-five per cent, from foreign countries. Of all tonnage entering the port, two-thirds was still sail-driven. Virtually no steam ships except mail packets worked the colonial trade but instead concentrated on the foreign and coastal trade. Approximately one-sixth of the tonnage was foreign-owned, giving some impression of Britain's dominance at sea.

Beyond the water highway, the ships and barges, the docks and warehouses, London provided also those very elaborate facilities, the commercial exchanges, which made the metropolis the world's greatest emporium. The Corporation of the City, the guilds, the Crown, and merchants themselves made systematic the ancient institutions which had provided general commercial exchange facilities. The first Royal Exchange had been given to London by Sir Thomas Gresham in the sixteenth century; the second was built after the Great Fire in the seventeenth century. Fire again destroyed the second in 1838, and the Corporation of the City, the Mercers, and Parliament contributed to the building of this third and last Royal Exchange. The building gives evidence that Victorian Englishmen wished to display ostentatiously their incredible economic success. Neither classical aristocratic nor functional simplicity satisfied the bourgeois pride.

The Royal Exchange provided the roof and the "walks" where economic negotiations could be carried on by men following the same business. If one group became so large that it needed more space or more specialized facilities, it left the Exchange for its own building. In 1802, for instance, the stock traders thought it expedient to leave the Royal Exchange and founded the Stock Exchange. Trading in stocks had grown enormously in the late eighteenth century, but also the stock traders in their daily frenzies disturbed all other functions in the old Exchange.

The Metal Exchange, already usefully setting world prices by example, stayed in the Royal Exchange until 1869. The Coal Exchange needed new facilities by mid-century and opened in 1849 a building making dramatic, experimental use of iron and a glass dome. The Coal Exchange had been a tight-knit monopoly, but in 1803 the City of London put an end to its exclusiveness. A totally free exchange dates from 1805, and this opening up of commercial facilities, together with the fantastically increased consumption of coal in the nineteenth century, explains the new building which occupied a site near the Billingsgate fish market where the medieval Hanse merchants had their "Steelyard."

The Old Corn Exchange handled grain and flour, the "New" Corn Exchange (a totally different operation), agricultural seeds. London had a Wool Exchange only from 1821, a fact which indicates the previous reliance upon domestic wool. Now, however, Australian imports particularly influenced the market. The Baltic Exchange (unlike the others mentioned) has a history quite separate from the Royal Exchange, though certainly it absorbed scattered trading from the Royal during the nineteenth century. The Baltic had a coffeehouse origin and came to specialize in the trading of whole shiploads of grain, tallow, oilseeds, and timber. Britain imported increasing quantities of all these products, but especially of timber from the early nineteenth century and grain from the 1850's.

The Foreign Exchange, dealing in currency, developed its functions largely in the nineteenth century, an obvious response to the complexities of British trade. The highly specialized and delicate business of dealing in gold, silver, and foreign currencies did not leave the Royal Exchange for new quarters but rather abandoned all central exchange facilities whatsoever in the twentieth century. The intricacies of currency dealings increased, and dealers established close, direct telegraphic and then telephonic communications with all major centers in the world. Such communications were possible from the 1870's.

"Lloyd's," one of the unique economic institutions in the world, also stayed at the Royal Exchange until the twentieth century. Originally an informal guild society of insurance underwriters meeting on coffeehouse premises, Lloyd's made formal its organization and techniques in the late eighteenth century and moved to the Royal Exchange in 1774. Only from the 1820's did financiers establish rival insurance firms, and Lloyd's needed considerable ingenuity to remain supreme in a difficult business. Lloyd's built "their" supremacy upon the underwriting of ships and cargoes, as the service of Lloyd's Registry of Shipping testifies, and whatever else Lloyd's eventually grew into, the firm established itself largely on the activities of the port of London.

Quite naturally, men of wealth in the City of London had for centuries lent money to the other men of enterprise, invention, and adventure. Every port of importance in the world had moneylenders or, by the nineteenth century, banks. But no other port, nor indeed nation, enjoyed access to such adequate banking facilities as were centered in the City of London. Since the late seventeenth century, the English government was inextricably involved with the growth of sound, dependable financial institutions. Relative financial stability in the eighteenth century encouraged industrialization, commercial enterprises overseas, and agricultural improvement at home. Men of wealth on the continent sent capital to England, where it drew lower interest but drew it regularly and with less risk of total loss.

The Bank of England had much to do with the soundness of English finance. Chartered in 1694 to help the government of William III solve its credit problems, the Bank immediately became first among supposed equals. It mobilized capital, held government debts as part of the developing credit system, gave strength and continuity to the whole structure of banking, helped to make the currency reliable, and survived (with frequent government aid) the many financial crises of the eighteenth and nineteenth centuries. Its governors and directors, men of enormous power and prestige, took their places among the elite or aristocracy who governed the nation from official, semiofficial, or private stations. Londoners of the nineteenth century had before them in the Bank one of the finest architectural pieces in the nation, apparently a masterpiece built between 1788 and 1808 by one of England's greatest architects, Sir John Soane. The twentieth century, not the Victorians, demolished Soane's structure during the 1920's and 1930's.

The Bank of England actively sought answers to the increasingly complex economic problems of the nineteenth century. Financial and commercial panic followed by relatively general depression struck Britain many times: 1815, 1819, 1825, 1847, 1857, 1866, and 1873. Time and again the Governors or the Courts of the Bank found they must make the difficult decisions which would destroy injudicious bankers and perhaps precipitate a crisis. The Bank judged the extent and pace of national credit, in theory responsible first to its own shareholders, increasingly then to all bankers who used the Bank, and ultimately to the voters and elite of Britain as represented in Parliament.

In short, the men of affairs who governed the Bank of England learned slowly and painfully that the institution which had been first among equals was becoming in the nineteenth century a central controlling bank. Many politicians, economists, bankers, and even men in the Bank itself flatly denied this new role, but while they denied it, all made use of the Bank as a central institution. Walter Bagehot, editor of the *Economist*, in the third quarter of the century brilliantly and energetically pointed out the trend to central control and supported it (especially in his book *Lombard Street*). No one, not even Bagehot, fully understood the role of a central bank, and inevitably the Bank found its affairs and its position debated vehemently in Parliament. Especially before mid-century the critical politicians raked over the power and influence of the Bank, but all men in government naturally sought national stability for money and credit. Consequently, they turned again and again to the Bank as the chief agency to achieve such stability. The Bank of England in 1808 received a monopoly on joint-stock banking (banks were in practice limited to six partners or less); smaller institutions in competition with the Bank supposedly would not upset intricate bank note issues.

In 1819, Parliament decided to return to full payment (convertability) in gold by 1821; though achieved, it did not prevent a major economic crisis in 1825. Some now saw smallness of provincial banks as a problem, and beyond a sixty-five-mile radius from London, the Bank lost its joint-stock monopoly. In 1833, Parliament made Bank of England notes legal tender, permitted joint-stock banks in London itself, and required the Bank to make monthly financial reports to the Chancellor of the Exchequer. The politicians thus contributed to a uniform currency, to extended banking, and to the public responsibility of the Bank, all in one blow. Then, in 1844, Peel's government passed into law one of the most important acts of the century, closely regulating the relationship of financial reserves and note issues. From this time the government did not interfere with the issue department of the Bank. The Bank became "the old lady of Threadneedle Street," above partisan politics, cautious, utterly responsible, sacrosanct.

The Bank also achieved its international status in the first three-quarters of the nineteenth century. It had attracted foreign capital since its foundation (Dutch subscribers were among the earliest), but what appealed to foreign creditors and debtors (especially, in the latter case, foreign governments) was the central nature of London's money market as controlled by the Bank. The great international financial houses such as Rothschild's, the huge City of London houses such as that of the Barings, and the joint-stock banks created at mid-century and after (many of them centered in the West End) watched the Bank of England and consulted her experts on foreign matters. The bankers of London preferred to venture their money in the huge loans which could be made to foreign governments; such loans provided large profits on very simple transactions. And as long as the British navy and the Foreign Office supported British interest in the Palmerstonian fashion, London bankers risked relatively little. British naval power could prevent governments from defaulting on loans, in other words. Historians have called such action "British intervention"; Victorians preferred to think about the sanctity of contract.

The Bank of France, with the highly centralized French economy and government at its disposal, threatened until 1870 to make Paris as important as London in the world money market. The Prussian defeat of France in 1870–71 ended that possibility, and London was supreme until World War I deeply compromised the British position. Unfortunately, after 1918 the financiers of London's successor, New York, did not understand the responsibility of being the world's money market; they took almost a quarter of a century to learn.

In one sense, London's international position in finance confirmed a weakness in the British economy. London's bankers only reluctantly provided some capital for industrial expansion; they infinitely preferred loans to foreign governments. As the Bank of England became the central institution rather than a largely commercial firm, the "country" bankers outside London relied largely upon the

City banks as intermediaries. Until the country banks became large by joint-stock operations, inadequate credit slowed industrial expansion. Thus, no source of capital provided funds for continuous industrial expansion. Later in the century the provincial banks themselves could invade the City, but by this time the great financiers had confirmed their preference for government loans. If some of the British capital which went overseas between 1865 and 1895 had gone into domestic industry, Britain's early industrial pre-eminence might not have been lost to the United States and Germany. Englishmen had themselves planted the seeds of relative economic decline even before the decade of the 1870's; sadly enough, London financiers bore a great deal of the responsibility. They perhaps held *too* much of a world view.

London bankers neglected industry; London was nevertheless the greatest manufacturing center of nineteenth century Britain. Writers frequently have misjudged London's position in industry, for virtually everyone thinks of industry in terms of the basic, mass-produced products of the so-called "Industrial Revolution": coal, metals, heavy machinery, and textiles. These industries centered in southern Wales (coal, iron, steel), Manchester and Leeds (textiles), Birmingham (machinery, specialized engineering, and metals), Glasgow (coal, shipbuilding, textiles), Newcastle (iron, coal, shipbuilding), and other provincial (and new) urban centers. Time and again, scholars and commentators point out that the stupendous industrial growth of the London area in the twentieth century represents a minor industrial revolution in itself.

In terms of production and employment, London surpassed all other industrial centers throughout the nineteenth century. In all major industries except metals and textiles London took an important place. With one-seventh of the total population of England and Wales living in London in 1871, one-sixth of the manufacturing workers lived there. One of every three workers in London was in manufacturing. The diversity of London's industries and the sheer confusion of the metropolis confounded most observers; they could more easily understand the relative simplicity of Manchester's cotton manufacturing, Leeds's wool, Cardiff's iron and coal, etc. Clothing, printing, precious metals and precision instruments, and furniture were London's ranking industries.

London had decided advantages for these and other industries. The port brought bulk goods at the cheapest possible rates; also, London, as the greatest emporium and the largest metropolis, provided a variety of goods, materials, and skills available no other place. London not only had the highest concentration of population, but those living in the metropolis (because of the Court, society, government) consumed goods at a more rapid rate than any other urban center in the kingdom. After the 1840's, as the British merchant marine outdistanced all other rivals and as Britain's free trade policy made London more attractive to merchants throughout the world, industry came to London in order to produce goods for transshipment to other markets. Finally, basic processing of some imports, notably food products, served other industries already located in London for other, earlier reasons.

Because of fashion, concentration of consumers, and plentiful supply of sweated labor, clothing manufacture stayed in the metropolis. Stepney (especially Whitechapel) held most of the small, sweated establishments which large-

ly made up the industry; the West End was a second concentration. Just after mid-century the clothing trade employed about 20,000 men and 100,000 women. When the
supply of sweated English and Irish labor ran low, a great
immigration of poor East European Jews provided a new
one. Perhaps the popularity of "ready-made" clothing after
1850 did most to expand the industry—and to keep it in
London in the twentieth century.

Printing boomed everywhere in nineteenth century
Britain, and though London, relatively speaking, lost
ground to provincial centers, she remained the most important single area for the production of books, printing of
newspapers, and commercial job printing. Earlier in the
century London probably employed more than sixty per
cent of all printers and related trades in the kingdom. By
1860, the proportion was fifty per cent, and it declined
slowly and steadily, to forty per cent in the 1950's. London's continuing dominance in intellectual life of course
attracted the whole process of book production, as well as
the lion's share of periodical printing. The City and Finsbury were particular centers of the industry.

The nineteenth century also saw the development of a
national newspaper press, though the real mass circulation
dailies appeared only in the 1880's. That privately owned
but semiofficial institution *The Times* conducted the successful experiments of the early century leading to steam-
driven cylinder presses; the railroads provided quick connections to the provinces. Parliament by inaugurating the
penny post (1839), repealing the newspaper stamp (1855),
repealing the paper tax (1861), and supporting the edu-
cating of the masses (especially after 1870) encouraged
further the expansion of printing.

Finsbury (Clerkenwell district) had the greatest share of the precious metals and precision instruments trade. The highly skilled artisans made jewelry, watches, clocks, compasses, and other instruments for ships, scales, and other measuring devices, and an enormous variety of specialized mechanical instruments. Competition outside London had already cut into these trades by 1870; foreign manufacturers (Belgian, German, Swiss) and Birmingham firms did their damage.

Furniture manufacturing, the fourth of the great industries of the metropolis, largely remained in the traditional areas (Shoreditch, St. Pancras, Bethnal Green, St. Marylebone), but already by the 1870's had indicated its future development toward mass production and a general move to the outskirts of London.

Enormously high real-estate value drove some industries from London. Engineering factories needed space, and they had gone by 1870. Only in Woolwich and Enfield, where the government had arsenals or shops, did important engineering works remain. For a variety of reasons the economic crisis of 1866 finished off a declining London shipbuilding industry. London produced both fine carriages and bulk wagons (vans) for dock work; the manufactory employed relatively few workers, however. Paint, paper products, food processing, and a variety of consumer goods also employed few workers, but these industries maintained good production.

Number Employed in Certain
Industrial and Mercantile Occupations, London, 1861

Clothing and Dress Makers	250,000
Food Processors and Related Workers	95,000

Builders (Carpenters, Masons, Bricklayers)	92,000
Shopkeepers, Sellers, Dealers	59,000
General Laborers	49,000
Textile, Cloth, Yarn, and Thread Workers	37,000
Metalworkers	34,000
Messengers and Porters	31,000
Carriers on Roads	30,000
Carriers on Seas and Rivers	30,000
Bookmaking (Compositors, Printers, etc.)	27,000
Furniture Makers	24,000
Woodworkers	18,000
Gardeners, Field and Pasture Workers	17,000
Machine and Tool Makers	13,000
Laborers with Animals	11,000
Coal Laborers	9,000
Watch and Instrument Makers	8,500
Papermakers and Related Trades	8,500
Shipbuilders	8,300
Carriers on Railways	8,000
Goldsmiths, Silversmiths, Gem Cutters	8,000
Stone and Clay Workers	7,000
Warehousemen and Related Trades	7,000
Gum and Resin Workers	6,000
Carriage Makers	6,000
Employed at Carving and Figures	6,000
Carriers on Canals and Rivers	6,000
Glass and Earthenware Workers	5,000
Musical Instrument Makers	5,000

The port, finance, industry: though the economic fundamentals, they do not provide for all of London. The metropolis also had thousands of shopkeepers living in rooms above their businesses and catering to the millions of inhabitants. It also had scores of thousands of domestic servants, and (to use Henry Mayhew) "those that will work, cannot work, and will not work."

Perhaps Hippolyte Taine best expressed in the 1860's the over-all impression of economic London: "Nothing here is natural: everything is transformed, violently changed, from the earth and man himself, to the very light and air. But the hugeness of this accumulation of man-made things takes off the attention from this deformity and this artifice; in default of a wholesome and noble beauty, there is life, teeming and grandiose."

The man-made things and the teeming, grandiose life provide fundamental ingredients for civilization.

III

Crown, Councils, and Corporation

POLITICAL LIFE filled Westminster, the "royal borough," as economic affairs filled the City. Neither excluded the other, of course, yet the government of England, of the United Kingdom, and of the Empire had settled itself almost two miles upriver to the southwest of the heart of the City. Government, indeed, characterized Westminster, along with the aristocratic social life so intimately related to government even in the mid-Victorian days of reform and liberalism.

Westminster as a city had no special pride, no liberties, no autonomous development which protected accumulated privilege. Westminster, the "West End," had become royal —to what extent one can still see simply by glancing at a map with the great stretches of royal parks (Hyde Park, Kensington Gardens, Green Park, St. James's Park, and Regent's Park). The national symbols of royalty, and consequently of government, were largely in Westminster.

The Tower of London was far downriver, below the City, but it was the symbol of a former royal tyranny and aristocratic capriciousness. The Tower in popular imagination was the setting for all that was "black" and "bloody." The myth of the Norman yoke, the myth which characterized the Normans as the destroyers of an Anglo-Saxon liberty which was only now being fully revived in Victoria's reign, pervaded the descriptions of the Tower in nineteenth-century guides, and enjoyed a surprising currency among Victorians of the middle and lower classes. But the more vital symbols of contemporary royal government were in Westminster: the palaces and the other government buildings.

Westminster Palace had served the medieval kings of England as their seat for the Michaelmas Court (one of three each year). William II in 1097–99 built the great hall which still strikes awe, and Richard II rebuilt it three centuries later. The ancient palace clustered itself around the Hall and the Abbey, a hodgepodge of additions, separate buildings, courts, and passages. Increasingly, the more formal functions of the Crown (law courts, councils, Parliament) were performed in the great Hall or nearby buildings. The fire of 1834 destroyed most of the Palace except the Hall, and the rebuilding is part of the story of Parliament, not of royal palaces.

Whitehall Palace succeeded Westminster as the seat of the king. Henry VIII's affection for palaces shifted as rapidly as his affection for women, but after Henry, Whitehall remained for the rest of the sixteenth century and most of the seventeenth the chief seat of England's monarchs, including Oliver Cromwell. Again, the Palace was a rambling collection of buildings centering around York House, the former London residence of the archbishops of York. The magnificent buildings of the Stuart era had long since disappeared even for the Victorians, for the fires of the late seventeenth century spared only the Banqueting House, a really superb piece of Inigo Jones architecture with Rubens-Jordaens ceiling paintings.

William III preferred Kensington Palace as his chief

residence, having purchased it from the Earl of Nottingham within a few months of the "Glorious Revolution" which brought Dutch William and Mary II to the throne. Christopher Wren made extensive changes to the Palace, which never became the official residence even though Anne, George I, and George II lived there. Members of the royal family, relatives, or aristocratic dependents have occupied the Palace since 1760. Victoria was born in Kensington and lived in the Palace until she became queen in 1837.

St. James's Palace shared royal honors with Kensington after the burning of Whitehall, serving as the site for levees, formal occasions, and many royal weddings. Royal decrees were issued from St. James's. Members of the royal family and favorites lived there, but St. James's was best known in the nineteenth century as the official designation for foreign representatives assigned to Great Britain. To eighteenth century Englishmen, and particularly to the intellectuals, politicians, and aristocrats of classical taste and oligarchical sentiments, St. James's symbolized the dangerous and insidious courtliness of the Stuarts. Baroque splendor and mannerisms masked tyranny. To Victorians, St. James's apparently meant largely the formalities of the Court of the Ambassadors, though Albert and Victoria were married in the Chapel Royal within St. James's.

But since Victoria's accession to the throne, Buckingham Palace had been the home and the major architectural symbol of royalty. A country house built by the Duke of Buckingham in 1705, it was owned by George III and then his Queen and then his eldest son, the Prince Regent. When the Prince became George IV in 1820, he decided to make his house the official residence. He commissioned Sir John Nash to begin the work which was not finished until the very year of Victoria's accession. Large but plain, and some would say even drab, the Palace gives one a sense of comfort on a grand and royal scale but an introspective sense of comfort which encourages one to believe more than one should in Lytton Strachey's portrait of a bourgeois Victoria. No quantity of George IV ostentation, appearances on balconies, elaborate railings, uniformed guards, Victoria Memorial, or radiating streets—all, of course, afterthoughts to the real purpose of the residence—have made Buckingham Palace much more than what it is, a country-house home for the royal family in the very middle of the metropolis where one was needed. It seemed as out of place in Victorian London as it does today, yet one cannot imagine London without it. The monarch, symbolizing with dignity the total structure of the constitution, was at home in Buckingham, but the governmental councils exercising the real power in the name of the monarch were to be found elsewhere. Buckingham Palace witnessed only the strict formalities.

Historical accident and royal personality, as well as principle and constitutional conflict, reduced the English monarch's direct powers. When Dickens was born, George III had already become totally insane. He had never been the villain which Americans and some English Whigs had painted, and he had helped to insure in a difficult era the continuity of responsible, if not always competent, administration. With George's insanity, the initiative went out of the throne for three crucial decades and consequently forever. The Prince Regent enjoyed his vices and left politics to his ministers. William IV, unbelievably dense of intellect, could only be troublesome. Victoria was too young, and only slowly did she and her German husband regain some influence in political affairs. But it was a personal sort of influence, as fragile as the interests, energy, or life of the monarch—or, as in 1861, as fragile as the life of the Prince Consort. Victoria, as the greatest of titled aristocrats, made suggestions, underlined emphatically and humorously her opinionated letters, and dispersed her favor and her disfavor. But, as queen, she of constitutional necessity was entirely passive: being informed, signing, reading speeches written for her, appearing in public, representing in flesh and blood the constitution of a nation and an empire. We do not yet know whether a flag or such a human representation has held more vital meaning for the mass of citizenry.

Real power, we have said, resided elsewhere, and this meant above all in the nineteenth century the Palace of Westminster, where the Great Council of Parliament sat. Until 1834 the Lords and the Commons met in relatively modest, crowded halls attached to the Palace, but then a fire destroyed the Houses of Parliament. In open competition the government accepted the architectural design of Charles Barry (actually the design was partially A. W. Pugin's in broad outline, and wholly Pugin's in detail) to replace the former Houses. Construction started in 1840, and in 1850 the Commons for the first time occupied the new quarters. The vast Gothic-revival pile henceforth represented London as much, if not more, than St. Paul's Cathedral or any of the great landmarks of the city. The new Houses of Parliament, into which Pugin poured his faith in the cultural necessity of Gothic architecture as the vehicle of Christian morality and ethics, became one of the most famous buildings in the world. After 1858 "Big Ben" sounded from the northern clock tower, adding another dimension to the fame of the building.

Parliament had in the early years of the nineteenth century achieved pre-eminence within the British constitution, but certainly it had not yet constructed that utter dominance which was characteristic of the 1860's and 1870's. At the close of the wars with Napoleonic Europe the House of Lords and the House of Commons, if not exact equals, enjoyed comparable status within the institution of Parliament. The Lords, for instance, provided the majority of cabinet ministers in every government until the 1850's. After 1858, except for a few months in one of Disraeli's governments, members of the House of Lords never enjoyed a majority in a cabinet. Such facts alone could mislead, however. Key members of any cabinet had to be in the House of Commons; incompetent peers with distinguished names could merely occupy ministries, and often did. In the first three-quarters of the century prime ministers from the House of Commons held power slightly more years than prime ministers from the House of Lords.

Membership in the Lords did not alone grant membership in the aristocracy. The peerage built a much broader base for itself during the eighteenth and nineteenth centuries, absorbing the brilliant, the monied, and the talented from among commoners. What mattered most in English society, and consequently in English politics, was a secure family base in landed, or "county" society: landed estates, a county seat, acceptance in county society. From such a base a family obtained one or more peerages and also found ways and means to win elections to the House of Commons for its younger sons and untitled talent. Peers could buy, or inherit, constituencies before 1832. After the Reform Act, the aristocracy relied upon influence to retain its political power; such influence had been at any time in British political history more important than outright purchase of parliamentary seats or bribery of the voters.

Obviously, the aristocracy included more than the titled peerage. Peers, their families and relatives, the gentry, many clergymen of the Established Church, barristers, naval and military officers, and even some academics had to be included, or at least seriously considered. Such diversity meant differences in attitudes and principles. For instance, the great peer with his huge estates and diverse interests would more likely be a Whig; the country squire, a Tory. Also, the wise peer or squire frequently invested in mercantile, mining, industrial, or financial enterprises. Agricultural income and land values boomed in the heyday of Victorian prosperity, thus tempting many landowners to invest too heavily in their estates, only to be led to financial ruin in the great agricultural depression of the 1880's. Yet in Dickens' era, the peerage and the landed aristocracy in general enjoyed wealth, prestige, and power, only slightly qualified by the challenge of the newer urban middle classes. The landed aristocracy for its titled members had an exclusive and powerful club in the House of Lords, and only a slightly less exclusive one for its untitled members in the House of Commons. Even the Second Reform Act of 1867 changed relatively little.

Dickens wrote an excellent piece of sarcasm on aristocratic politics in his own time, in *Bleak House*, ch. XL:

> England has been in a dreadful state for some weeks.
> Lord Coodle would go out, Sir Thomas Doodle wouldn't

come in, and there being nobody in Great Britain (to speak of) except Coodle and Doodle, there has been no Government. It is a mercy that the hostile meeting between those two great men, which at one time seemed inevitable, did not come off; because if both pistols had taken effect, and Coodle and Doodle had killed each other, it is to be presumed that England must have waited to be governed until young Coodle and young Doodle, now in frocks and long stockings, were grown up. This stupendous national calamity, however, was averted by Lord Coodle's making the timely discovery, that if in the heat of debate he had said that he scorned and despised the whole ignoble career of Sir Thomas Doodle, he had merely meant to say that party differences should never induce him to withhold from it the tribute of his warmest admiration; while it as opportunely turned out, on the other hand, that Sir Thomas Doodle had in his own bosom expressly booked Lord Coodle to go down to posterity as the mirror of virtue and honour. Still England has been some weeks in the dismal strait of having no pilot (as was well observed by Sir Leicester Dedlock) to weather the storm; and the marvellous part of the matter is, that England has not appeared to care very much about it, but has gone on eating and drinking and marrying and giving in marriage, as the old world did in the days before the flood. But Coodle knew the danger, and Doodle knew the danger, and all their followers and hangers-on had the clearest possible perception of the danger. At last Sir Thomas Doodle has not only condescended to come in, but has done it handsomely, bringing in with him all his nephews, all his male cousins, and all his brothers-in-law. So there is hope for the old ship yet.

Doodle has found that he must throw himself upon the country—chiefly in the form of sovereigns and beer. In this metamorphosed state he is available in a good many places simultaneously, and can throw himself upon a considerable portion of the country at one time. Britannia being much occupied in pocketing Doodle in the form of sovereigns, and swallowing Doodle in the form of beer, and in swearing herself black in the face that she does neither—plainly to the advancement of her glory and morality—the London season comes to a sudden end, through all the Doodleites and Coodleites dispersing to assist Britannia in those religious exercises.

The manner in which the aristocrats used their power was in itself a clue to their resiliency through centuries of English politics. Unlike the excessively arrogant and aggressively privileged aristocracy of eighteenth-century France, which largely deserved its fate after 1789, the English aristocracy rarely lost its sense of political balance in the nineteenth century. As a class both in the Lords and the Commons, it gave way slowly when pressures built up from the *bourgeoisie*, the artisans, or the new urban centers. Only in 1831, over reform of the House of Commons, did a large portion of the Lords threaten to resist to the threshold of general disorder.

The anomalies of the old electoral system caused many aristocrats themselves to support reform in 1832. Decade after decade, radicals castigated the "Norman tyrants" (i.e., the peers), implied threats to the House of Lords, and talked of "the Peers against the People." Politics, however, were not so simple; only a truculent, economically hard-pressed, politically unwise House of Lords in 1911 finally brought on a major reform of the constitution which limited the role of the Lords.

The Lords, then, preferred no open conflicts with the masses, or with the Commons. Brilliant demagogues from the Commons such as Henry Brougham could be smothered with the heavy honor and prestige of a peerage. Lord Brougham did not pose the threat to privilege that Henry Brougham had. Themselves recognizing the intricate blend of responsibility and privilege which gave them their position in English society, the aristocrats gave up or restricted some of their prerogatives. The Church of England, which in the eighteenth century had been turned into an adjunct of government for the economic, social, and political use of the aristocracy, won some independence and regained some moral fervor after the 1820's. Likewise the Empire, while never an exclusive preserve of the aristocracy but still a convenient dumping ground for embarrassing aristocrats, was increasingly professionalized and thus bureaucratized. The aristocracy's strangle hold on the universities also was eased. By 1870, inherited privilege alone did not guarantee one power and influence. Education had become the key to the civil service, the church, imperial position, and politics.

But, of course, the aristocrats had the interests and the resources to guarantee for their sons the best education in Britain, and perhaps in all of Europe. To a significant degree, the educated elite of late Victorian Britain was largely the old aristocracy in more appealing guise, and with some new recruits. Before 1870, new wealth became respectable if translated into land; respectable education for the sons only enhanced the position of the family. Thus, the Peels moved from industrial wealth to respectability. The father of the great prime minister, Sir Robert Peel, provided his son with landed wealth, education at Eton and Oxford, a seat in the House of Commons, and a comfortable income from the cotton mills—an unbeatable combination considering the high intelligence and extensive talents of the son. Increasingly in the last half of the century, aristocrats must also prove themselves in the examination halls at Oxford, Cambridge, and (sometimes) London, almost regardless of their inheritance.

After the decade of the 1820's, with subtlety and rarely in precisely measured strides, the House of Commons assumed political initiative and absorbed the prestige and power of Parliament. More in Pugin's Gothic surroundings than in the old and temporary buildings housing them before 1850, the Commons made itself into a forum for the representatives of all segments of British society. The ruling classes did not guarantee equal representation to anyone; such to most great politicians of the era was irrelevant. They considered "democracy" anathema, synonymous with the excesses of the continent and most especially France—and synonymous also with corrupt, demagogic politics of the United States.

Yet it was fitting that broad representation should be granted slowly by the aristocrats who dominated Parliament. Articulate industrialists, businessmen, clerks, dissenting Protestants, and workingmen spoke up in newspapers, in the great public meetings characteristic of the era, and in a variety of printed matter. Such was "public opinion," and Britain's governors listened to it, even if reluctantly.

Step by step, national attention focused on the House of Commons. Begrudgingly, the Commons from the 1820's allowed a printer, Hansard, to report its debates, printing an unofficial but relatively complete account. Newspapers also printed brief reports. By the 1860's and 1870's public attention focused on the House of Commons as never before. The formation of two distinct parties, Liberal and Conservative, after 1865 sharpened and simplified the issues for public consumption. The political duel of Gladstone and Disraeli dramatized the shift of influence to the House of Commons.

Politicians channeled most of this "public opinion" into respectable political institutions as the century passed. Clever men, and even principled men, learned how to focus public anxiety and excitement to their benefit. This was nothing new, but the particular institutionalization deeply influenced world affairs. George Canning made public opinion a component of British foreign policy; Palmerston used it brilliantly and cynically. The public meeting and mass outdoor demonstration first frightened Britain's aristocrats, but again they learned how to manage the committees, unions, leagues, etc., behind the great agitations and pressure campaigns. Political parties absorbed them, at the same time preserving the supposed "independence" of the original organization.

Victorians so formalized the politics of mass pressure that one historian has spoken of the "ritual" of the public meeting. The more perceptive political leaders, some of them with great reluctance, tightened the organization of political parties. Parties became the channels (and also the neutralizers) of public opinion. Peel and Disraeli in particular, the former with positive distaste, did much to inspire and direct the growth of political parties. They institutionalized party machinery, particularly finances, selection of candidates, propaganda and registration, and located the institutions in London as much as possible. Other poli-

ticians—John Bright and Gladstone most clearly—ignored
party institutions but used their immense talents of sway-
ing crowds to achieve some continuity of political purpose.

The House of Commons in some ways became the victim
of its own mythology. Supposedly the locale for open and
unlimited debate on any question, parliamentary business
piled up and up and up by the 1850's and 1860's. While
conditions at home and in the Empire complicated the
governing of such a vast realm and while men with all sorts
of interests looked to Parliament for action, the Commons
seemed less capable of ordering itself. On any really important issue, Gladstone or Disraeli was expected to speak
four or five hours, and any member of the House who
wanted to talk must be allowed to do so. Individual members also were trapped by both the new and the old political
techniques. Constituents and nonconstituents still presented
petitions for redress of grievances to M.P.s, who in turn
must present them to the House. No one believed petitions
of any genuine consequence in Victorian politics, yet all
feared to cease going through the traditional motions. Men
frequently place great stock in gestures.

Likewise, M.P.s now courted their constituents as never
before and of necessity had to spend precious time away
from Parliament at the organized public meetings. Political
parties as we know them in the twentieth century were
developing, but not yet could they be protective buffers for
the hard-pressed M.P. Naturally, such a situation also added
to the vitality of the Commons, for neither could parties
manipulate the individual M.P. Parliament was nearer at
hand for the voters in the 1860's than at any time since
that decade.

In short, Barry and Pugin's magnificent and utterly successful piece of monumental architecture served as a grand theater, in which the House of Commons seized the attention of the British public. The Commons, like any good theatrical company, provided its moments of high drama, its tragedy, its low comedy, its farce. In the previous century the actors had performed largely for themselves; in Victoria's century they performed instead for those not in the House.

To put it another way, in the eighteenth century the Commons turned furiously on the "stranger" reporting its debates. In the nineteenth century, M.P.s said everything with a thought for the omnipresent public.

The general public, more truthfully the voters, and more truthfully still the elite, produced the endless array of parliamentary dramatic pieces, both major and minor. The directors were the ministers of the Crown, themselves a part of it all by constitutional necessity. They sat in Parliament.

Like so much else about this government, men and events had not yet worked out cabinet rule as the twentieth century knows it. Eighteenth-century politics left the significant legacy of the office of the "prime minister" with extensive powers to be used as the occupant judged best. In general, the prime ministers in the first six decades of the century thought of themselves as first among equals, allowing their ministers great individuality of political principle and administration. The prime minister tried to keep his various cabinet members working together as best he could, but not yet was there "collective responsibility"—the doctrine that a whole cabinet, the government, was responsible for the significant mistakes of a single minister.

Not yet did political principle mean more to politicians than continuity of administration. Perhaps it never does.

However, deep feeling, new interests, and even passions did on occasion intrude themselves into the cozy world of the elite. We have seen how public opinion influenced politics through various techniques, but also this demand for earnestness and intent (even when self-interest was largely involved) placed a premium by the 1860's on ministries with seemingly coherent and consistent principles. Peel from 1841 to 1846 led a government to which, even if accidentally, he gave energy, *esprit de corps*, and coherence. Disraeli and Gladstone did much more consciously to stamp political affairs with coherent principles, and with them after 1865 we decidedly enter the world of the "-isms": in this case, Conservatism and Liberalism. Gladstone with his deep reserves of real and faked moral righteousness probably left a more obvious hallmark on the late Victorian political alloy.

The leaders of all political parties (contrary to mythology, there were always more than two before the 1860's) faced each other across the aisle in the House of Commons. When we talk of the administration guided by the ministers in power, however, we change locales. North of the Houses of Parliament in Whitehall the administrative offices clustered themselves.

Many Victorian writers emphasized "the obscure *cul-de-sac*" of Downing Street and the eighteenth-century modesty of No. 10 in order to magnify the greatness of the British system. Few prime ministers in the nineteenth or twentieth centuries have actually lived in No. 10. In Dickens' lifetime only the Earl Grey (1832–34) did so. Most prime ministers, being men of means and social prominence, owned substantial town houses of their own. No. 10 they used officially for offices, cabinet meetings, etc. Behind the simple front of No. 10 existed more than a modest town house, as one might suspect though few writers mention. A larger house, a garden, and openings to the other official houses nearby made the whole complex a good deal more than adequate, even if not princely. Such cautious elegance could not really be understood by the Victorian *bourgeoisie*, who wore their wealth on their buildings in garish decoration and then boasted about the "proper" modesty of the prime minister's house. The middle class constantly talked "retrenchment" (economy in government).

More truly each decade, No. 10 became the cockpit of governmental power. Looming around it were the great blocks of buildings which housed the growing administrative structure. The Treasury Buildings, an accumulation of construction dating some of their bits even from the Tudor era, had been given a uniform façade in the 1840's. The Buildings served largely as a massive secretariat to the offices of the first lord of the treasury (the prime minister) and the chancellor of the exchequer in Downing Street. The Privy Council, the Home Office, and the Board of Trade were located there.

South of Downing Street, at least until 1864, the old Foreign Office sprawled. Then the whole area was cleared, and the vast government offices in (at Palmerston's demand) Palladian style were constructed from 1868 until 1875. The Foreign Office, the India Office, and the Colonial Office occupied the new block. Thus, the bureaucracy busy with home and economic affairs had settled into quarters north of Downing Street; the bureaucracy managing imperial and foreign affairs, south.

North of this administrative complex and still on Whitehall the Horse Guards housed until 1856 most offices having

to do with the Army, but the furor over military ineffi-
ciency in the Crimea caused the government to rationalize
the civilian administration of the Army in the office of the
secretary of state for war. The War Office then moved to
Buckingham House in Pall Mall Street, the commander in
chief remaining at the Horse Guards. The Paymaster General's Office flanked the Horse Guards to the north, and
still farther along stood Admiralty House and the Admiralty. Significantly, the Admiralty was most distant from the
officialdom of the ministries, for it maintained a dignified
independence—even a remoteness—which Britain's political
leaders and civil servants respected.

Victorians knew well one other government building
which was nowhere near Whitehall, namely Somerset
House. Commenced in 1776 on a site near today's Waterloo
Bridge, the enormous structure was intended to house
governmental offices of all kinds. In Dickens' lifetime the
Audit Office, the Office of the Registrar-General, and the
Inland Revenue Department gradually crowded out other
departments. In the vaults of Somerset House civil servants
stored the vital statistics (births, deaths, marriages, wills)
of Victorian Britons. Until mid-century the building also
housed royal societies, but the removal of the Royal
Academy in 1856 ended the more obvious patronage-
support for such groups. They acquired their own quarters
and left Somerset to the bureaucrats and the students
of King's College. The bureaucracy represented one legacy
of Benthamite rationalization of government; King's represented an orthodox, traditional response to such rationalization.

Dickens gave both politicians and civil servants their
share of satire, sarcasm, and irony, but nothing he ever

wrote was as viciously effective as the passages on the Court
of Chancery, lawyers, and legality in *Bleak House* (ch. I):

> London. Michaelmas Term lately over, and the Lord
> Chancellor sitting in Lincoln's Inn Hall. Implacable
> November weather. As much mud in the streets, as if
> the waters had but newly retired from the face of the
> earth, and it would not be wonderful to meet a Mega-
> losaurus, forty feet long or so, waddling like an elephan-
> tine lizard up Holborn Hill.
>
> . . .
>
> Fog everywhere. Fog up the river . . . fog down the river.
> Fog on the Essex marshes. . . . Fog creeping into the
> cabooses of collier-brigs; fog lying out on the yeards . . .;
> fog drooping on the gunwhales of barges and small boats.
> . . . The raw afternoon is rawest, and the dense fog is
> densest, and the muddy streets are muddiest, near that
> leaden-headed old obstruction, appropriate ornament for
> the threshold of the leaden-headed old corporation,
> Temple Bar. And hard by Temple Bar, in Lincoln's Inn
> Hall, at the very heart of the fog, sits the Lord High
> Chancellor in his High Court of Chancery. . . .
>
> Never can there come fog too thick, never can there
> come mud and mire too deep, to assort with the groping
> and floundering condition which this High Court of
> Chancery, most pestilent of hoary sinners, holds, this day,
> in the sight of heaven and earth.

Though reformers of all varieties realized the need for
judicial reform in Britain, relatively little had been accomplished. As the Utilitarians, following Bentham, had said,
English law had merely accumulated for centuries. Precedent was confused, and the judiciary was a fantastic con-

fusion of overlapping jurisdictions. Peel as home secretary in the 1820's accomplished some codification of real importance.

The judiciary, however, remained untouched until the very end of the 1860's. The various courts sat at Westminster (in the various buildings clustered around the old Hall) or at Lincoln's Inn, causing the legal profession great inconvenience in shuttling back and forth between Westminster and South Holborn. Lawyers and others pressed numerous schemes for a consolidation of the courts, but only in 1868 did the government finally begin to build the Law Courts on the Strand near St. Clement Dane's Church. Construction went on for fourteen years. Likewise, the great Victorian reform of the judiciary came finally in 1873, heralded by a century of debate and theoretical writing. Historians are still trying to assess the impact Dickens' *Bleak House* had on this judicial reform.

The Inns of Court, the centers of the legal profession and consequently closely related to the judicial functions of government, were also in South Holborn. The Inner Temple, the Middle Temple, Clement's Inn, and Lincoln's Inn presented to Victorians their traditional collegiate character. Law students still occupied rooms in the Inns; more barristers lived in; the bombs of the 1940's had not yet destroyed great chunks of the Temple and Clement's Inn. Even without the Law Courts, London had a legal quarter which straddled the eastern boundary of the City and thus spread into Holborn. In 1866, the government added to the quarter by opening the new Public Record Office in Chancery Lane to lawyers and "antiquaries" (i.e., historians). For the first time, officials collected under one roof (a Gothic one, of course) vast quantities of governmental records. What the ministries of Whitehall accumulated in the form of paper thus came to be catalogued and stored in Chancery Lane.

By contrast, government of the United Kingdom and the Empire seemed divine reason as compared to the government—rather, the *governments*—of London itself. Only a highly imaginative reader could picture the sheer disorder which characterized the whole urban area. Continental travelers, and particularly the French, talked of the chaos which was London.

Gradually, matters improved. After Sir Robert Peel established his Metropolitan Police—first called "Peelers," and then "Bobbies"—in 1829, at least a centralized office worked to preserve peace and order in an area including all of Middlesex, and all parishes which had any boundary within fifteen miles of Charing Cross, and no boundary more than eighteen miles from Charing Cross. Replacing in all areas except the City and the "Liberties" the few and ineffective watchmen or "Charlies," the "Bobbies" rapidly but discreetly grew in number.

In 1839, the Metropolitan Police took over the Thames Police, formerly under the City. By the year of Dickens' death the Metropolitan Police force numbered about 7,500 men with headquarters in Scotland Yard. "Scotland Yard" had in fact become synonymous with the police; gradually the Police Headquarters displaced other offices and private homes in their famous area. Britain had no national police, and consequently the Metropolitan Police provided help and advice to the counties, boroughs, and cities all over the kingdom. London, after all, included one-fifth of the population of England, and an even larger percentage of the population fell within the Metropolitan Police District. It perhaps could not be said in 1870, as it can be today, that London was probably more orderly than most urban or rural areas of the country. Still, public attitudes and the police had remarkably changed London in forty years.

Britain's leaders agonized over London's government throughout the nineteenth century. Before 1888 they accomplished very little, and only in 1899 did Parliament finally impose some logic on the chaos of authorities throughout the metropolitan area. Above it all, the City remained aloof and relatively untouched. How did the City escape the reforming zeal of nineteenth-century Britons? Through economic and political influence, British respect for charter and contract, politicians' ignorance of urban complexes and their problems, and politicians' fear of creating in any London-wide government a virtual state-within-the-state rivaling the national authority.

A simple explanation of the City's government is bound to be misleading, but a detailed account would serve no purpose here. Four major councils, or "courts," governed the City. At the lowest level, all ratepayers within the ward (the City had twenty-six) belonged to the "wardmote," which managed ward affairs, elected the alderman (with only freemen voting), and nominated freemen to the Court of Common Council. If a ballot was required after the nominations, then only freemen could vote. A ratepayer could only become a "freeman" of the City through one of the livery companies. The City of London had eighty-one livery companies (descendants of the medieval guilds) in the nineteenth century. The "Twelve Great Companies"— the guilds with most members, influence, and wealth—were the Mercers, Grocers, Drapers, Fishmongers, Goldsmiths,

Skinners, Merchant Tailors, Haberdashers, Salters, Iron-mongers, Vintners, and Clothworkers.

The Court of Common Council, next highest of the four councils, was early in the century composed of the lord mayor, the other twenty-five aldermen, and about 199 common councillors elected by the wards. After 1840 the City reformed the election of common councillors and allotted 206 seats among the various wards. The Common Council managed the property, income, and taxation of the City and generally thought of itself as the "House of Commons" of the City. With such powers it claimed many more—again not unlike the Commons.

But the Court of Aldermen, the third great council, maintained its dignity and powers. It dominated the City's representation in the Commons (four M.P.s), oversaw elections of all kinds, admitted to all offices, made payments from the treasury, and maintained judicial powers. Most aldermen functioned as justices of the peace and many actually held commissions.

The fourth court or council was the Court of Common Hall, or the general court of lord mayor, aldermen, and all liverymen of the City. This court, so important in the past, did little in the nineteenth century. It nominated two aldermen for the office of lord mayor; the Court of Aldermen elected one. It elected the two sheriffs of London each year (they also served jointly as sheriff of Middlesex) and also elected four annual Auditors of the Corporation accounts. On occasion, the Court of Common Hall made other general claims to authority, but it had lost out in the shuffling for place among the various medieval bodies in which the nineteenth-century City reveled.

93

At the head of it all was the lord mayor, elected by his fellow aldermen for one year, during which time he consulted with ministers, represented to the nation the enormous economic power of the City, served as the most active magistrate, presided over the courts, and constantly participated in the elaborate ceremonies. He worked with virtually no staff.

The City employed a host of officers, both ill-paid and overpaid. The list makes one imagine that virtually all freemen of the City were officers of one sort or another, yet the corporation did have extensive functions. It was until 1857 the Conservator of the Thames, as we have seen; fortunately, Parliament intervened to reform this aspect of City power. Within a radius of seven miles the City owned a monopoly of markets, and within twelve miles it collected coal duties. Within the City itself in 1848 the corporation created the "Commissioners of Sewers," trying to modernize local government services somewhat. Even though the commissioners took control of sewers and pavement, many of the previous functionaries continued to be appointed.

Parliament nibbled at the City's often obstructive power in one other important way; in 1855, it created the Metropolitan Board of Works with supervisory powers over building. In 1858, the board gained power to construct systems of main drainage on both sides of the river, and from 1864 the board carried on the Embankment of the Thames.

Except for the metropolitan-wide reforms (Metropolitan Police, Conservancy of the Thames, Metropolitan Board of Works), not much was changed outside of the City, either. A welter of vestries (sixty-four parishes outside the City, some of them subdivided), unreformed and reformed but almost always viciously inefficient, governed the remainder of the metropolis except for Westminster, which was technically a royal city with a "Court of Burgesses." Actually, the magistrates governed Westminster, and the ratepayers were largely quiescent. Because the central authority filled Westminster with its palaces, halls, and ministries, it usually had more of the conveniences of urban life than the City. The "parliamentary boroughs," designated by Parliament for the election of M.P.s only, had no functions which could be carried over into local government. Between 1832 and 1867 (the dates of the first and second reform bills) London had twelve Members of Parliament: four from the City, and two each from Westminster, "Tower Hamlets," Finsbury, and Marylebone. After 1867 London received another two seats for Chelsea, and the University of London received one.

In short, the total situation oozed confusion and futility. The City should have taken the lead and organized a metropolitan movement which could still have preserved City rights and privileges. The City, after all, was the economic heart of the metropolis and more responsible for London's very existence than Westminster. Instead, the City had no leaders during the nineteenth century with sufficient foresight and imagination to lead in such a direction—"the leaden-headed corporation," Dickens had called it. The aldermen were wealthy and comfortable and had other interests. They had no particular desire to change anything, except perhaps the traditional dominance of the landed classes. The common councillors were shopkeepers, shopkeeper-artisans, petty businessmen, or lesser professionals and cared about little except their corner of the mass which was London. Shopkeepers and their like, in fact, controlled

London in the nineteenth century: a laudable fact for the City itself but disastrous for the whole metropolis. The great financiers and merchants princes abandoned the City during the century, as did the workingmen. The City's population steadily declined.

As for the other districts in the metropolis, no one had the prestige or the influence to lead the metropolitan area. With forty-one per cent of the population in 1861 in Middlesex, thirty per cent in Surrey, and twenty-nine per cent in Kent, the situation remained triply confused. The vestries were, before the 1830's, largely the worst examples of "democracy" or were closed and self-perpetuating (and perhaps corrupt). Even when the vestries were open, reformed, and responsible, men of means and ambition saw no benefit in participating in local government. Thus, in the end the central authority *gave* London a metropolitan government; London did not develop one of her own. The London County Council challenged men of ability as the vestries never had; the metropolis, two decades after Dickens' death, finally had thrust upon it opportunities for enlightened local government for one-fifth of the kingdom's population.

IV

Enormous Pleasures . . .

LEIGH HUNT spoke of London's "enormous experience of pleasure and pain." London's pleasure, interpreted most broadly, made the metropolis one of the greatest cultural centers of the European world. A historical account of pleasures, particularly when one employs the noun "culture," is a hazardous enterprise. Cultural heritage includes very largely the refinements of taste: in other words, what we often narrowly and sometimes arrogantly assume to be the best a society is able to produce.

Before the nineteenth century what the elite considered pleasurable or best pervaded society: the *bourgeoisie* accepted these values and largely imitated their betters. The merchants and lawyers of Swift's or Pope's or Johnson's England knew their places, their limits, and the aristocratically established paths (marriage, land, politics) to higher social status. Culturally, the landed aristocracy established themselves at the apex of a pyramid, and the lower orders recognized aristocratic supremacy in taste and position.

Bourgeois attitudes changed somewhat in Dickens' century, however. Some of the middle classes exuded a confidence unknown before. Rich, or at least prospering, the English *bourgeoisie* frequently demanded cultural pleasures on their own terms, and imposed some of their concepts of culture on the rest of society. Along with middle-class morality, middle-class taste influenced all levels of society. London witnessed less of this social revolution than Birmingham, Manchester, or Leeds. On the other hand, the identifiable aristocratic and working-class legacies set distinct bounds to the *bourgeoisie* in London. One can see the social and cultural limitations on the so-called "rising" middle class in Victorian society.

Class tastes and class consciousness, consequently, directed London's cultural life. In important ways English urban life, and most especially London's life, suggested the mass culture of the twentieth century. The aristocracy set the pace, as always, but now the *bourgeoisie* demanded—and got—qualifications on their own terms. As for the working classes, cultured society forgets about their culture or cultures as quickly as it can. Working-class culture has been smothered in the silence of written evidence, absorbed and made "responsible" or "respectable" by the elite, or simply ignored by those refined classes which largely preserve the evidence on which any historical account must be based. What is more, Leigh Hunt's "pain" (poverty, epidemics, illness, crime, filth, prostitution) qualified the cultural achievement, and such pain the working classes largely suffered.

Londoners of all social classes shared few pleasures except coronations, royal weddings, and the like; even then they experienced these entertainments in distinctive, class-governed ways. Aristocrats held their balls and great dinners; the middle classes enjoyed illuminations and public dinners; the working classes drank free beer. Londoners of any status did not usually, after all, experience their pleasures in view of all. "Public Pleasures" include, rather, those experiences more pleasurable, without any particularly recognizable cultural intent, and engaged in more or less publicly, or openly, with one's peers.

All London could enjoy the parks. Fortunately for the metropolis, the Crown had carefully guarded its "estates" in the West End. Since the seventeenth century the Crown, while strictly preserving its residual rights, opened Hyde Park and St. James's Park to the general public. Until the nineteenth century the parks remained bits of wild, or relatively wild, country, with uncertain paths, wild flowers, untrimmed shrubs, trees, and grass. The Prince Regent's planners largely made the parks "picturesque" with formal ponds, careful paths, defined gardens, gates, railings, and the like. Still, the Regent left his parks decidedly casual as compared to those of the Continent.

The aristocracy used Hyde Park as an outdoor stage upon which to show off their clothes, their escorts, their horses, and their carriages. Anyone with social pretension must of absolute necessity be "seen" on the "Row" at whatever society prescribed for the moment as the proper time. No place else in London could an observer in such a short space of time see so many of the fashionable and the would-be fashionable. They also strolled in St. James's Park, supposedly to see the birds and fowl which the Crown had kept there for centuries, and they rambled in the Royal Botanical Society Gardens in Regent's Park. But in Hyde Park they rode, surveyed, and were surveyed.

Aristocrats also enjoyed Hyde Park for other of their sports and pleasures. Until mid-century an occasional two- or three-horse race for a bet occurred. Dandies took out boats on the Serpentine, skated on ice when they could, fought duels as late as the 1820's, or pretentiously drank water from one of the several wells scattered through the park. The Crown held military reviews in the park on the grand occasions of the century, and from the 1850's the Volunteers (a pathetic gesture towards "the nation in arms") drilled there.

Lesser folk enjoyed the parks increasingly in Victoria's reign. Thousands of the poor swam in, or splashed in, the dirty waters of the Serpentine in the early decades. They and the middle classes could hire boats by mid-century. On Sundays, in particular, the *bourgeoisie* and near-*bourgeoisie* (artisans and shopkeepers) showed their best clothing on walks in Hyde Park, Regent's Park, and St. James's Park. Aristocrats frequently protested the presence of "rabble," particularly in St. James's Park during July and August when many fashionable families were "out of town." Gradually, Hyde Park witnessed an "understanding" of classes, in which the aristocracy seldom claimed precedence on Sundays. The fact was, however, that the Royal Parks were slowly but surely becoming public parks for "breathing in," as one writer in the 1870's put it. Also, the Sunday crowds drew speakers and hucksters to Hyde Park, providing a new element of education and entertainment.

The general public encouraged the development of the Zoological Gardens in Regent's Park. The Crown kept a royal menagerie in the Tower until 1834 but then transferred the animals to the Zoological Society Gardens which had been established in 1828. From mid-century the zoo expanded rapidly, and visitors increased even more rapidly. In its own rather peculiar way, the collection of animals reflected Britain's expanding imperial and commercial interests. As the British Empire incorporated new territory, or as new trade treaties were negotiated with sheiks or rajas or chiefs or sultans, the zoo acquired new animals. The masses had little chance to enjoy much else about Regent's Park except the zoo, at least before Primrose Hill to the north was developed as a sort of "peoples' park" and annexed to Regent's Park.

While the Crown and the aristocrats shared the West End open areas with the less fashionable, the working classes had before the 1860's only one park exclusively theirs. Victoria Park in the East End began to develop out of a government purchase of land in 1840. Then the government began to develop the two square miles of Battersea Park, south of the Thames, for the common people. The government established three other parks in quick succession in the 1860's: Alexandra Park to the far north in 1864, Southwark (Rotherhithe) Park in 1865, and Finsbury Park in 1866. To the north Hampstead Heath remained a preserve of the well-to-do during Dickens' lifetime, but then working-class pressure to use the Heath hardly existed so early. Far to the west, Londoners could also use royal lands at Kew or Richmond, but they found them unnecessarily remote at this time.

Visitors to London made one interesting point about the parks. Englishmen seemed not to enjoy the open space simply by sitting and relaxing out of doors. Quiet sitting was not the Englishman's way. He rode or walked vigorously and with some sort of purpose even if that purpose was to be seen fashionably. He wanted to watch some activity, if not engage in it himself. In short, he wanted to do something in the parks, not just be there. The people transferred to the parks the restless activity which pervaded the metropolis all week. Frenchmen, in particular, noticed their nervous energy in swimming, boating, riding, walking, bird-watching, playing at games, bowling, or what-have-you. They always had in mind the contrast to the parks of Paris, where people lounged, relaxed, and watched other people.

Though one might have seen very considerable working-class activity in the parks, the people's pleasure had by mid-century become something of a problem in the metropolis. In previous centuries local fairs in and around London, and then the street fairs in the built-up areas, provided the lower classes with recreation. Entertainers of every sort set up booths at the fairs; no one performed first-class dramatic works in the nineteenth century, as they had in the eighteenth, however. Jugglers, puppeteers, acrobats, animal trainers, singers, magicians, and the like entertained the crowds. Skits of one kind or another abounded. Men, women, and children could see wrestling, fist-fighting, and animal-baiting, even though the constables might oppose these entertainments in particular. Venders sold food, clothes, and everything else under the sun—including stolen goods. The authorities knew it and opposed such illegalities where they could. They usually could not control a fair once it got under way, a situation which encouraged them to think of doing away with the fairs altogether. Originally, fairs had animal shows and major entertainments, but the remaining street fairs of Dickens' time were largely street markets on a large scale.

The upper classes, for many reasons, did not approve of the fairs. The Corporation of the City had market rights for the metropolitan area and found fairs exceedingly difficult to control in terms of market rights. Crime and rowdiness also centered on fairs; respectable public officials and their enforcement officers took steps against all the fairs.

Bartholomew's Fair, perhaps the most famous, died a relatively quiet death in 1855, having been bled persistently for three decades by local authorities. By this time all the fairs were gone, except for occasional gestures in the suburbs (Clapham, for instance) where new housing collected around ancient villages. Street markets evaded the authorities; Petticoat Lane continued to function, for instance, as an important old clothes market in spite of occasional harassment by constables and magistrates.

The lower classes developed other entertainments. By 1870, London had 20,000 "pubs" (public houses) catering largely to the working and lower middle classes. Fortunately for the health of the people, beer replaced gin as the working-class drink; drunkenness declined stupendously in the second and third quarters of the century. And, incidentally, abstemious evangelical prohibitionists and temperance leaguers took, and have since been granted, too much credit for this important social change which is not yet fully understood. Many of the pubs gave music to their patrons, as any reader of Dickens will know (the Sol's Arms in *Bleak House*, for instance). All in all, in the working-class pub of the nineteenth century, as well as in the country inn, the much admired pub of today finds its origins. In spite of pious middle-class "temperance" movements (a hypocritical label, since they worked for *prohibition*) which fought the "liquor traffic" and restricted opening hours, a congenial and comfortable, and even democratic, institution developed.

Well-to-do workers, their families, and some middle-class families patronized another institution which had not yet shown its full vigor by 1870. The "music hall" (more than four hundred were licensed) provided variety enter-

103

tainment (skits, comedy, songs, dancing) not unlike that in some of the fancier pubs, but without the beer. The halls grew larger and larger; three were large enough to hold betwen 15,000 and 20,000 each, but most were far smaller. In the music-hall tradition, particularly, the working classes supported a musical and theatrical development which is frequently a good deal more attractive, and perhaps more important, than most of the deadening legitimate theater of the early Victorian era.

The more comfortable and privileged classes enjoyed their equivalents of these working-class entertainments. The Corporation of the City seemed often in the Victorian era to be largely one huge, elaborate dining society. On any good excuse, such as the visit of a foreign dignitary (Garibaldi in 1864), at any traditional occasion (the annual lord mayor's banquet), and even on the flimsiest excuses, the leaders of the Corporation of the City paid for banquets. Besides the city government, political parties, well-heeled pressure groups, interest groups, societies, leagues, committees, unions, councils, etc., institutionalized the public banquet. Some great leaders honed their oratorical talents on diners. Gladstone, for instance, learned on banqueting tours that he had a crowd-pleasing ability to speak. He moved on to great mass meetings and came close to demagoguery in some of his efforts. Here was entertainment with a purpose. In London the Guildhall or one of the separate halls for a guild served as the site for such affairs.

Until mid-century London had at another level of well-to-do entertainment, its "pleasure gardens," the most famous being Vauxhall, south of the river. The Prince Regent gave Vauxhall its last years of upper-class popularity; after his death the place declined steadily until auctioneers sold it off in 1860. Going to Vauxhall was naughty, perhaps a touch adventuresome, but not totally scandalous even in its last years. Higher-priced prostitutes strolled in the formal gardens, but the gardens did not exist simply to provide a less sordid locale than the Haymarket for the well-to-do to buy their women. Londoners who could pay the substantial admission price to the pleasure gardens could see formal gardens, fountains, fabulous lighting, mock ruins, Italian arches, colonnades, pavilions, copies of famous statues, and the authentic representation of William Tell's cottage. They witnessed dancing, theatricals, balloon-ascents, and fireworks. They gave balls, took supper, had tea, drank punch, and watched the crowds. By the 1840's even some artisans could afford entrance to Vauxhall. The fashionable abandoned it, except for occasional slumming; it closed in 1859.

Besides the glitter of aristocratic society, particularly during "the season" of February to July when everything (including Parliament) happened, the fashionable had their clubs. Pall Mall and St. James's, in the heart of the West End, were the chief sites, then as now. Each served some sort of group which had similar professions, similar social connections, similar politics, or similar pretentions.

The professional and middle classes rapidly expanded the list of clubs in Dickens' lifetime. He himself was a member of the Atheneum, where (it was hoped) men of outstanding literary and professional talents could talk with each other but also could meet and talk with political leaders. Perhaps more than any other of the prestigious clubs, the Atheneum brought together the talent of the complex society which Britain had developed by mid-century:

Dickens, Thackeray, Ruskin, Darwin, Sedgewick, Grote, Tyndal, Huxley, and Macaulay among the intellectuals or writers; Shaftesbury, Disraeli, Granville, and Sir John Bowring among the politicians; Bishop Wilberforce, Bishop Thirlwall, and Dean Stanley among the Churchmen; Serjeant Kinglake and Sir Edwin Landseer among the artists. The Atheneum, like other clubs, provided members with a library (the Atheneum reputedly had the best), lounges, a good dining room, and in general the services and surroundings of a grand aristocratic "salon" which few of them could otherwise afford. Dickens came from decidedly lower middle-class background; his talents brought wealth and social acceptance very rapidly. At the Atheneum the man who as a child of twelve worked in a blacking factory and visited his family in debtors' prison (Marshalsea) matched wits with men of better birth.

Other clubs attracted their own special sort of men. The Carleton drew in the great Tory leaders; the Reform collected Liberals. The Army and Navy had obvious clientele, as did the Oxford and Cambridge. The United Service Club had members who were royal princes, military and naval officers (including militia), and lords lieutenant of the counties. In St. James's the older aristocratic clubs which had one time specialized in gambling (White's, Boodle's, Brook's) sat near new clubs of distinctly middle-class membership.

In the same category as the clubs, but far more socially exclusive than any club dared be, was "Almack's Rooms." Also located in St. James's, Almack's was perhaps the most exclusive organization in all of Britain. Not surprisingly, really, for its six high judges were women—"Lady Patronesses." Here in season on each Wednesday, that special quarter or so of the aristocracy which was acceptable to the six ladies enjoyed magnificent balls under the strictest of management. At least writers of the time said that three-quarters of the aristocracy was unacceptable to Almack's. Commercial wealth, or new wealth of any sort, stained a candidate irreparably and prevented membership. Victoria's England let the institution fade and die; Willis's Rooms, infinitely less exclusive, succeeded Almack's. After all, it was Lady Palmerston, once a tyrannical "lady patronness" of Almack's, who later elaborately praised (even if for political purposes) the middle classes.

In a category by itself, as far as public pleasures are concerned, is the Great International Exhibition held in London in 1851. London's and all of Britain's public made the exhibition as successful as any world fair could hope to be. For Englishmen the exhibition became a landmark of the century, for it emphasized the progress which Victorians hoped to be an absolute law of history (at least English history). The year 1851 marked the economic progress of three-quarters of a century and pointed to the expected prosperity of the future. In fact, Britain was just entering a quarter of a century of unequaled prosperity.

Prince Albert identified himself with the project from the first. Most major politicians initially opposed the whole idea. The Queen appointed the Royal Commission in January, 1850. In March the Lord Mayor of London invited the mayors of all important British towns to the inevitable banquet at Mansion House. The Prince explained the project to the mayors, indulging in fewer superlatives than any other speaker or writer on the subject for the next quarter of a century. All comments on the exhibition, then as later, foresaw peace, international understanding, free competition, and eternal progress as being immensely well served by such an event.

No one, including Albert, foresaw the scope of the project. Immediately, the commissioners realized that no building or group of buildings in London could possibly contain such an exhibit. After considerable controversy and discussion the commission accepted the "Crystal Palace" plan of Joseph Paxton, the Duke of Devonshire's gardener. Paxton proposed a building of iron and glass, more than four times as long as St. Paul's Cathedral and twice as wide; in brief, he suggested a monstrous greenhouse or conservatory which had uncalculated impact on modern architecture because of the unique combination of materials. The commissioners probably accepted Paxton's plan because the very idea of having to pay for the removal of a building of brick or stone from Hyde Park staggered them.

Two thousand workmen finished Paxton's practical piece of fantasy in about five months. Victoria, Albert, and virtually every living British notable opened the exhibition on May 1, 1851. Journalists who described the opening outdid themselves; they could, in another era, have been splendid emotional scenario writers for Cecil B. DeMille. Trumpets, cannons, royal troops, cheers, waving hats, fountains, organs, seven hundred choristers, flags: opening day had them all. Englishmen became, and remained, uncharacteristically emotional about the whole enterprise.

Then the first of the 6,000,000 visitors began to tour the 19,000 exhibits arranged in four general categories: Raw Materials; Machinery and Mechanical Inventions; Manufactures; and Sculpture and Plastic Art. The promoters had collected the greatest array of machine-made items yet seen by men. Viewers could plainly see British pre-eminence, though the quality of some French, Belgian, and German goods was too easily ignored. Since 1851, industrial societies have struggled to preserve handicrafts at exhibits; in 1851, the excitement and pride centered on anything machine-made, even if badly made.

Hyde Park saw the last of the Crystal Palace in 1852, but Londoners did not lose the great hulk. It was purchased by several entrepreneurs, modified, and set up near Paxton's home in Sydenham, a southeast London suburb. In what was a more respectable situation for Victorian gentlemen and *bourgeoisie*, the Crystal Palace took the place of the pleasure gardens of the past. Surrounded by elaborate, ostentatious, garish gardens with fountains which one calculated in terms of water usage rather than in terms of art, the Palace provided a shelter for a mishmash of Victorian culture. The managers built Egyptian, Greek, Roman, Assyrian, Medieval, Renaissance, Italian, French, Spanish, Pompeian, Bohemian, and Ceramic "courts"; they later added others. A visitor could see life-size models of dinosaurs, a geological exhibit, tropical gardens indoors, an exact replica of the Alhambra's "Court of Lions," a model of the Danish fortress of Duppel in 1864, and other exhibits created for the headlines of the day. An aquarium, lectures on cooking, a library, a reading room, afternoon concerts, popular plays, readings, pantomimes, seasonal shows (the annual Christmas exhibit was particularly famous), concerts, and talks also filled the annual programs. The Handel Festival started in 1857 and the Triennial Festival in 1862. In 1866, a Christmas-season fire destroyed the tropical gardens and the Assyrian Court; it was a foretaste of the total destruction of the great monument seventy years later.

Londoners retained other assets from the Great Exhibition, too. Prince Albert and other interested men established at Marlborough House in 1852 a museum which displayed objects purchased from the exhibition. The museum also took in the collections of the Government School of Design. It then, over several years, went through several changes of name and purpose. Dickens knew the museum as the South Kensington, around which the International Exhibition of 1862 was organized. It flopped badly. From 1871 the commissioners of 1851, still spending the profits of that year, organized specialized exhibits to encourage design, fine arts, and manufacturing. The accumulation of various collections, along with this whole tradition of the Great Exhibition, became the Victoria and Albert Museum of today.

Legitimate theater did not serve nineteenth-century Londoners with particular distinction, but then, Londoners apparently demanded little or nothing of it in return. The accounts of the era leave one with the general impression of deadness: uninspired playwrights, ham acting, sloppy productions, an ignorant public, and foolish government regulations. The music hall with its skits, songs, and farce seems the more persistent, vigorous tradition. What is more, fanatical amateurs such as Dickens gave more life to theatricals than many of the professionals.

Until 1843, only three theaters received licenses for spoken drama or "legitimate" drama. Undoubtedly the government stifled some innovation and excellence by such control. The control in an unfortunate manner did encourage innovation of a sort. When the unlicensed theaters wanted to produce Shakespeare or Restoration drama or new plays, songs had to be interjected to satisfy the law.

But one might point out that some of the greatest and most impressive productions of sixteenth-century plays in the twentieth century have brilliantly included music. However, producers seemed content to put together mishmashes of entertainment; the public expected nothing more.

The Drury Lane Theatre, burned in 1809, was rebuilt to hold nearly 3,000 people. The producers and managers of the theater allowed a steady decline of quality, primarily because the other general theaters and music halls cut into Drury Lane's clientele. Particularly after the Kemble family (John Philip Kemble, Charles Kemble, and Mrs. Siddons) left Drury Lane for Covent Garden in 1803, London's aristocrats went to Drury Lane more for the associations with high society than for quality of drama. Drury Lane presented light opera (*very* light, from the sound of it), farce, burlesque and "burlettas," some plays, and an occasional English classic.

Covent Garden contributed slightly more in this era. The Kembles superbly acted and produced plays after their coming to the theater in 1803. In 1808, the theater was destroyed by fire (every theater was seriously damaged or utterly destroyed by fire at least once in each generation). When Smirke's new building was opened in 1809, the theater enjoyed considerable success for three decades. Occasional Shakespeare, classical English comedies, English opera, and some new plays dominated the bills; then in the 1830's Covent Garden produced Shakespearean plays frequently. The public responded positively and thus encouraged a general revival of Shakespeare in other theaters.

In the 1840's Covent Garden tried Shakespeare, classical Greek plays, pantomimes, and some of that general mishmash entertainment previously mentioned. Attendance declined, however, perhaps because of national economic difficulties. In 1847, Covent Garden decided to break the monopoly of Her Majesty's Theatre on Italian opera. By simply ignoring the monopoly and calculating that Lord John Russell's "liberal" government would not enforce it, Covent Garden moved decisively into a new phase of its history. A fire destroyed the theater again in 1856, and Barry's new structure incorporated by design the best features from continental theaters for the production of grand opera. With seating for 2,000, the new Covent Garden opened in 1858 with Meyerbeer's *Les Huguenots*.

The third licensed theater, Her Majesty's in the Haymarket (at least with a back entrance on the Haymarket), had before 1847 such a monopoly on Italian opera that Londoners referred to the theater as "The Opera House." Formerly the King's Theatre, its directors had introduced Mozart's operas to the London public in the years after 1806. In 1818–19, Nash and Repton reconstructed the theater, which then produced some extremely popular operas starring Madame Grisi and other great singers of the day. Covent Garden's invasion of Her Majesty's sole right to produce opera did not at first do serious damage for one major reason. In the 1847–49 season Her Majesty's featured Jenny Lind, who collected such rabid fans that her very name became an operatic legend throughout Europe. Critics, sometimes caustically, referred to the "Lind mania" in London. After it was over, the theater declined steadily for almost two decades. Fire destroyed the building in 1867; naturally, the proprietors and directors hoped to rejuvenate the theater with a new building. They failed. Though almost finished, the new theater did not open for the 1869 season, nor for several years afterward. Ironically, but appropriately, Moody and Sankey used the building for their American-style religious revival in 1875. Since revivals on such a scale are, above all else, intricate dramatic performances, Moody's efforts may well have been among the best theatrical productions in nineteenth-century London.

The end of exclusive licensing in 1843 aided other theaters in London. In the quarter of a century or so which followed the change, about a dozen theaters of various sorts attracted a reasonably large public. The Haymarket Theatre, rebuilt by John Nash in the 1820's with that handsome front and seating for almost 15,000, specialized in classical English comedy (Restoration and eighteenth-century, particularly) and new plays. Macready (Dickens' close friend), Charles Kean, and Ellen Tree (Mrs. Kean) always attracted sizable audiences. In the same category of theaters, the Princess's Theatre on Oxford Street gave a great boost to the Shakespeare revival by allowing Charles Kean to produce Shakespeare's plays for an entire decade (1849–59). Likewise, Sadler's Wells Theatre, growing out of Sadler's Music Hall at Islington Spa, changed its history drastically by presenting over thirty Shakespearean plays beginning in 1846. Samuel Phelps produced the plays, which apparently were more popular than any other Shakespeare revivals of the time. Before Phelps, Sadler's Wells largely presented that mixed bag of entertainment seen elsewhere. Londoners identified this theater with Grimaldi, the greatest clown of the century, who worked there from 1818 until 1828.

Lesser theaters developed specialties. The Lyceum, which in 1802 had first housed Madame Tussaud's wax exhibit, produced light opera and later some Italian opera. The Adelphi and the Olympic did melodramas. The Vaudeville presented exactly what its name indicates and was really a particularly pretentious music hall. All of these theaters were in the Strand or its vicinity.

The Gaiety opened in 1868 to introduce Parisian *opéra bouffe* to London. South of the Thames, the Royal Coburg Theatre became the Royal Victoria Theatre in 1833. Henceforth, it was for all London "the Old Vic." Not usually presenting anything of much distinction (even though Paganini performed there in 1834), the theater declined rapidly until it became after 1871 a particularly poor music hall. Astley's Theatre, also to the south, was really a circus ring for "equestrian dramas." St. James's Theatre in the fashionable club district largely produced French and other continental plays.

Beyond the theaters, licensed or not, a great many theatricals existed: small theaters or halls, music halls, pubs with entertainment, and even street entertainment. Even the wildest imagination would be hard pressed to make the era really important to the British theater. London freed the theater of many restrictions and revived Shakespeare. Otherwise, what mattered most was the new respectability which the theater won. Gradually the *bourgeoisie*, or the "middle classes," who simply had no place in the scheme of eighteenth-century British society and consequently were left out of so much, patronized the theater. Theaters became more than resorts of drinking rowdies, prostitutes, and aristocrats—of course, they had been more than this before, but "respectable" Londoners had not thought so. The middle classes wanted culture; they hungrily sought roots in the English past and in "good taste." They could afford to patronize the theaters after 1850 and felt it not morally degrading to do so. By the year of Dickens' death, then, London theaters had a much enlarged potential public upon which to build incredible diversity and excellence during the next century.

Vocal music attracted Londoners as did no instrumental music. Opera was a persistent attraction, as we have seen. Performances of oratorios, recitals, and concerts of religious songs drew regular and large audiences. Englishmen seemed peculiarly addicted to the monstrous choirs which performed at festivals or on religious occasions. One suspects they would have organized every single Englishman, Welshman, and Scotsman on the island to sing Handel's "Hallelujah Chorus" in harmony, if it had been at all feasible. Choirs, organs, and accompanying orchestras grew larger and larger during the century. The Sacred Harmonic Society performing under Joseph Surman at Exeter Hall in the Strand collected choirs of around 700 at mid-century. When the Crystal Palace had been moved to Sydenham and was available, organizers mustered thousands of choristers. The first Triennial Festival in 1862 featured 3,120 voices and 505 instrumentalists. At the Fifth Triennial Festival in 1874 more than 4,000 performers roared forth Handel, Mozart, and Bach. Choral societies abounded in London, as all over England, and no well-meaning organizer had difficulty in finding numbers of voices.

Englishmen liked all vocal music, not only encouraging oratorios and Italian and English opera but expecting *gentil* songs for entertainment on social evenings. Any well-bred lady sang a little and played the pianoforte a little. "A little" indeed, the public discouraged professionalism. Really first-rate musicians, conductors, and composers had to be imported. The aristocrats dallied with things musical but did not give sustained patronage which encouraged important, long-range development of the musical arts. English attitudes toward professional musicians is excellently illustrated by George Eliot in *Daniel Deronda*; they were at best odd, arrogant, and probably foreign. Virtually any Victorian novel suggests on the other hand the good breeding, with musical accomplishments, which society expected of a young lady.

Until 1848 the subscription Concerts of Ancient Music (anything over twenty-five years old was defined as "ancient") popularized Mozart and Haydn for the aristocratic few. For large orchestral pieces London had only the Philharmonic Society organized in 1813. The society first held its concerts in the Argyll Rooms, Regent Street, then in Her Majesty's Theatre, and then in the new St. James's Hall where Dickens often read his works after 1858. It sponsored Beethoven, Mendelssohn, Weber, Berlioz, and Wagner in England, but the public accepted only Mendelssohn fully. It doubted the others.

Many writers have commented on the tendency of the English public to give utterly uncritical, even irrational adoration to the occasional composer. The worship of Handel was, and remained, a national mania. The admiration of Mendelssohn flared intensely for a time but then mellowed somewhat. He first visited London in 1829 and returned frequently.

As for English composers in this era, they were hardly worth even a word of rejection.

In 1823, aristocratic amateurs organized the Royal Academy of Music. In 1845, aristocrats and musicians established the Musical Union for chamber music. In 1859, Monday Popular Concerts widened the musical public slightly. But all in all, one can relate little about music of much importance. London's musical offerings were just exactly that—musical offerings. With the possible exception of Sir Michael Costa, most conductors were mediocre immigrants who could not have made their way on the Continent. Costa helped to prepare the ground for major work in the generation after 1870, but English interests and tastes became more cosmopolitan, too—and more demanding. Victoria opened the Royal Albert Hall of Arts and Sciences in 1871, and thus London finally had a large (6,000 to 8,000 seats, depending upon whether a choral work was being performed or not), convenient, relatively acceptable concert hall.

As for Dickens' contemporaries, one suspects that too many of them would have felt the greatest musical event of the generation to have been the opening of the Great Exhibition of 1851, when an obviously emotional Victoria strolled through the Crystal Palace to the cheers and hat-waving of thousands, the noise of at least three organs, and the crescendo of many musicians and voices rendering "God Save the Queen" and the inevitable "Hallelujah Chorus."

Compared to the eighteenth or previous centuries, nineteenth-century cultural life relied uniquely on formal institutions. Some writers state far too simply that a "rising middle class," hungry for culture but unable to obtain or afford it except collectively, caused the growth of important cultural institutions. Certainly the increasing number of prosperous Englishmen supported cultural activities throughout the kingdom, and nowhere so obviously as in London. And certainly a larger and larger *bourgeoisie* "acquired" cultural tastes, at first copying the aristocracy but then aggressively asserting its own taste as it asserted its morality. The total picture is of course a complex one—

more complex than a mosaic because the pieces vary infinitely in size and color. The wealthier *bourgeoisie* copied the aristocracy; the professional *bourgeoisie* (writers, journalists, civil servants, teachers) often refined and deepened aristocratic taste; the lesser *bourgeoisie* distorted and frequently cheapened everything, but at least they shared in cultural achievement.

The aristocracy also participated in the elaboration of formal institutions which had cultural intent. The new world of Victorian England complicated the relatively straightforward cohesion of the eighteenth-century landed aristocrats. They now had a variety of economic interests; politics became a more serious game; London grew in size and complexity and kept the old aristocracy from its easily managed habits of social-cultural-political life. Consequently, even the aristocracy needed formal institutions. Also, new tastes in music, as we have seen, forced changes. New seriousness about art and education also demanded new institutions. As London life for a man of any socioeconomic class became increasingly complex and diverse, formal institutions became even more important to all Londoners with taste or pretense of taste.

In museums and libraries Londoners displayed increasing interest during the century. This interest seems far more tangible than that in music and drama, but probably because the collections of paintings, sculpture, objects of art and science, and books can be calculated more precisely than quality of drama and music. One can immediately name two undisputably great painters of nineteenth-century England, Constable and Turner. British scholarship, literature, and science contributed much to European civilization. Victorians sustained the British genius for architecture (latter-day cynics notwithstanding). Music and drama could not match such achievements.

As with music, though more significantly, London's experience with art both widened and deepened from 1800 to 1870. Eighteenth-century aristocrats ostentatiously collected paintings and some sculpture; frequently other aristocrats or indeed any "respectable" petitioner could view the houses and collections resulting from the accumulated fortunes of centuries. However, the viewing public was small.

Most artists did not easily win respectability in either the aristocratic eighteenth century nor the more diverse nineteenth. Obviously successful painters could be tolerated; they were patronized and even lionized if they painted flattering portraits. In such a situation, Sir Joshua Reynolds tried to institutionalize and canonize taste and respectability in the Royal Academy founded in 1768.

Neither vicious, jealous, nor brilliant critics brought the academy tumbling down in Dickens' lifetime, though frequently they gave it a good shaking. The annual exhibits (*"the* Exhibition," to knowing Londoners) remained the chief artistic event of any season. The academy held its exhibits at Somerset House, its official home, until 1837. Then it used the National Gallery in Trafalgar Square from 1837 until 1868, after which time Burlington House became permanent quarters. As for its meetings, the academy used Somerset House until 1856 and then moved on to the National Gallery, followed by the move to Burlington House.

The academy obviously encouraged portraiture at the expense of landscape painting. In the uncertain realm of artistic judgment the academy scored modestly high in its selection of good artists for membership or associate membership. Critics, of course, remembered the utterly hopeless artists instead. At least three of the five presidents of the academy during these seven decades have maintained modest reputations: Benjamin West (until 1820), Sir Thomas Lawrence (1820–30), and Sir Charles Lock Eastlake (1850–65). Sir Martin Archer Shee (1830–50) and Sir Francis Grant (from 1865) have fared poorly.

As a meaningful artists' association, the academy failed in the nineteenth century. Reynolds also failed to create dogmatic standards of public taste—and had actually failed before the nineteenth century. Academicians and Associate Academicians went their separate ways in the vast metropolis. They did not carry on either a direct or indirect dialogue in the academy. Most were fashionable and perhaps earnest—but not earnest enough for the young rebels of the century. Though constantly flayed by a multitude of critics during the century, the academy remained aloof, respectable, and often dull. But consistently so.

Cliques of artists, as with similar groups in most other nations, founded societies during the century. Thus they tried to achieve that exchange of ideas and inspiration which, supposedly, artists enjoyed. The most famous such clique of nineteenth-century London was the Pre-Raphaelite Brotherhood, which managed to absorb a host of disciples even though no one could define its ideals. Reality, self-expression, poignancy united the Pre-Raphaelites—and all other artists, for that matter. If for no other reason or influence, the Pre-Raphaelites stirred up first the nasty attacks upon their work, and then put up a spirited defense. Coming after public controversy over Turner's art, the exchanges served the cause of art handsomely by publicizing artistic ideals and dedication.

Prices paid for art soared upward because of public interest and general prosperity as well as controversy; thus a lively commercial exhibitors' trade supplemented institutional exhibitions. Several commercial galleries collected in Pall Mall, near the haunts of the fashionably wealthy. Also, the British Institution, founded early in the century by wealthy patrons, exhibited private collections and new work. The Institute of Painters in Water Colours fought against the general prejudice against their genre but made very little headway during the nineteenth century.

Prince Albert aided artists in several ways. He bought paintings and prints for the royal collection; naturally, he acquired some trash and perhaps rather more than necessary. He also arranged important exhibits, such as that of the collections of Prince Ottingen-Wallerstein at Kensington Palace in 1848. He supported the National Gallery when he could see how to do so (and it was exceedingly difficult in the maze of criticism) and lent that invaluable support of 1850–51 to the Great Exhibition. Mixing together as it did both junk and objects of real merit, the exhibition encouraged public patronage of art and design. A lasting result of Albert's interests was the South Kensington Museum, already mentioned in association with 1851.

Virtually every writer about Victorian painting mentions Albert's encouragement of exhibits of medieval and Renaissance art, but Albert alone did not lead his wife's subjects to such new interests. Aristocrats exhibited their collections in rented halls (Lord Ward's exhibit in the Egyptian Hall, Piccadilly, in 1851, for instance, which featured medieval pieces), used the British Institution early in the century, and then loaned exhibits to the South Kensington Museum from the late 1860's. Cardinal Newman's, Thomas Carlyle's, A. W. Pugin's, John Ruskin's, and William Morris' varied but vigorous bolstering of things medieval (in opposition of course to "liberals," Radicals, utilitarians, freethinkers, etc.) sharpened public interest in history and art. The public took the next step to the Renaissance easily, since Victorians were if anything eclectic.

The National Gallery and the South Kensington Museum both have figured in our discussion. The National Gallery originated in 1824 with the government acquisition of the Angerstein pictures. Smirke finished his extremely controversial building on Trafalgar Square in 1837; already it was inadequate to house the purchases and gifts. In 1851, Turner left the vast accumulation of his own work to the Gallery; by this time the situation was ridiculous. Everyone had a scheme for a new gallery or some sort of arrangement. In its own way, the debate proved a growing public interest in art. After 1868 the removal of the academy to Burlington House reduced, but did not eliminate, the problems of the National Gallery.

To what extent the public used the National Gallery is hard to fathom. Snobs protested the presence of laughable, middle-class Philistines; bourgeois Radicals from the north of England thought such national expense regrettable when so few used the gallery. Other writers described the steadily increasing traffic in the gallery and remarked on the mixture of aristocrats, foreigners, and *bourgeoisie*.

The South Kensington Museum, later the Victoria and Albert, developed as we have seen—that is, out of the Exhibitions of 1851 and 1862. No one doubted the traffic in it;

obviously the variety of exhibits brought in significant crowds. Rotating exhibits of medieval and Renaissance art, textiles, glass and ceramics, prints, jewelry, the Raphael Cartoons, the Museum of Patents, the "Science and Art Department," full-size reproductions of famous art objects of Europe, non-European art, the National Portrait Gallery, and costumes filled room after room of the complex. The museum was essentially the first major institution to be located in South Kensington, which became known as virtually an institutional quarter in the last three decades of the century. In 1873, for instance, workmen started the building for the natural history collections of the British Museum, but the collections were not moved until 1881.

Away in Bloomsbury the British Museum developed in Dickens' century into an institution of colossal proportions and importance. Like the South Kensington Museum, though earlier, the British Museum more or less accumulated without any special purpose. The government purchased Montagu House in 1754. Sir Hans Sloane's natural history collections formed the initial acquisition. The Harleian Library of Manuscripts, the Cottonian Library, and George III's royal library of 120,000 volumes opened up new paths for accumulation. Then in the early nineteenth century the Townley Collection of Antiquities and the Elgin Marbles provided yet another dimension for the museum.

From 1810, approximately, the Trustees of the Museum opened the collections more freely to the public—at least to the "respectable" public. They extended hours and privileges and finally built the great dome for the Reading Room. By 1870 the museum reportedly held 800,000 volumes and perhaps 600,000 manuscripts of all types. The

Copyright Act of 1843 officially recognized the pre-eminence of the museum as a national depository for published material. Finally, by mid-century the newspaper collection acquired London, provincial, Scottish, and then Irish newspapers. The trustees rarely planned far enough ahead of such growth, but the removal of the natural history collections to South Kensington in 1881 relieved some of the pressure.

The "B.M." of course eclipsed all other libraries in the metropolis. The clubs kept small libraries, and London had its specialty libraries (such as Dr. Williams' Library, composed of 30,000 volumes on dissent). Such libraries largely served the very few. The London Library, opened in 1841 as a subscription and lending library, provided books on learned subjects for circulation. By 1870 the library had 80,000 volumes, and a very large clientele from the aristocratic, middle, and professional classes. For the less learned reader, Mudie's Circulating Library at the corner of New Oxford Street and Museum Street was the fiction book club of the era. In 1870, Mudie's supposedly had 800,000 volumes on hand or in circulation, many of them duplicates of course. Mudie's selection of novels could make or break the marginal novelist or temporarily salvage the waning one. Scores, and probably hundreds, of lesser imitators of Mudie's catered to the immense popularity of fiction and travel accounts. Here, and probably only here, one has a very middle-class institution of sorts.

The word "Victorian" usually evokes thoughts of religious piety, moral earnestness, and puritanical hypocrisy. Such judgment contains half-truths, or perhaps a bit more. If religious piety requires worshipful devotion to God, intense loyalty to the forms and content of religious services, and subjection of one's habits to the generally accepted religious customs, then Victorians were not pious. Victorians did not concern themselves especially with religious questions: that is, they had learned to live with and to accept theological diversity and tended (with some important exceptions) to de-emphasize religious forms and habits. Victorians of all persuasions did, however, devote themselves to moral earnestness: that is, they were deeply and perpetually concerned about the moral health of society, about human actions which touched most directly upon the lives of other members of society. I am making the distinction between the worship of God (religion) and the human responsibility, perhaps religiously based and perhaps not, to other human beings (morality).

Moral earnestness finally became the dominant attitude of Victorians. Slowly but steadily, middle-class evangelicalism ate away the more relaxed, sometimes robust morality of the eighteenth century. John Wesley began the attack upon the aristocracy and its loose habits which, in his opinion, qualified its position of natural leadership. He did not suggest replacing the aristocracy but instead urged its moral regeneration. Ironically, Wesley's attitudes immediately infected the middle classes, only slightly touched the aristocracy, and very momentarily brushed the working classes.

Wesley was simply the most important single objector in the widespread reaction to and criticism of rationalistic thought. Middle-class sects—that is, virtually all the nonconforming Protestant groups—underwent major changes in the late eighteenth century and were again infused with religious enthusiasm. Evangelical enthusiasm also entered the Established Church; William Wilberforce and his well-to-do friends, who lived in Clapham, and were thus called the "Clapham Saints," opened the Anglican door to middle-class earnestness. They thus prevented the nonconforming sects from gaining a total monopoly on the new enthusiasm. Even the Roman Catholics through such converts as John Henry Cardinal Newman and William Cardinal Manning were influenced by the new moral earnestness. Newman's upbringing had been in an evangelical household. Manning, like his good friend Gladstone, was a peculiar mixture of High Church Anglicanism and Low Church enthusiasm before he converted to Catholicism—and afterward, too, as far as that went.

The moral earnestness which came to be called "Victorian," even though it originated earlier than Victoria's reign, enforced a decidedly bourgeois morality: abstinence, seriousness, self-improvement, discipline, moral courage, forbearance, providence, duty, truthfulness, perseverance, fastidiousness, industry, thrift, energy, and punctuality. Such bourgeois morality gradually captured the aristocracy and consequently became the enforced standards of society. At most points of contact, evangelical morality complemented "liberalism," which was essentially the nineteenth-century refinement of Enlightenment principles. Both evangelical morality and liberalism underlined the crucial theoretical importance of the individual. But where the principles of liberalism conflicted with bourgeois morality, as in the case of evangelicals' demanding that the state intervene to prohibit alcoholic beverages and liberals' hesitating to use the state in such a fashion, then bourgeois morality ignored liberalism. By the end of the nineteenth century both were dead or dying as vital forces in British life. Liberalism tore itself to pieces trying to resolve the dilemma

of its suspicion of the state versus its genuine desire to further humanitarian causes. Evangelical morality became
priggery.

As for puritanical hypocrisy, critics of the Victorians
force too much upon them. Victorians defined the ideal of
moral behavior; few of them lived up to such rigorous
standards. For instance, the presence of 80,000 prostitutes in
London did not prove that Victorian morality was auto-
matically hypocritical. A substantial opposition to bourgeois standards maintained itself throughout the nineteenth
century and found a public champion, of sorts, in the
Prince of Wales during the 1860's. The future Edward VII
already made hash of the generally accepted moral code
more than three decades before his mother died.

Such unrealistic standards as those of bourgeois morality
encouraged men to seem publicly to conform to the norms,
it is true. Aristocrats without the slightest intention of
conforming to such standards kept up a public front; after
all, the middle classes gained considerable political power
during the century and had to be given their due. Men
could not always live comfortably with such rigorous
standards, and when they failed to live up to them, then the
intolerance of Victorian society led them to devious and
hypocritical behavior. Perhaps Victorian standards begot
more hypocrites than many moral systems, yet "hypocritical" is not the foremost adjective to apply to the whole
society. Demanding, intolerant, narrow, and idealistic
might be better words to describe it properly.

Nor was the society smug. Victorians were neither self-
satisfied nor complacent and thought nothing certain except
the need to be morally earnest. All else seemed doubtful,
even the idea of progress. Oscar Wilde played with the

fundamentals of Victorian society when he punned on *The Importance of Being Earnest*.

By the middle of the nineteenth century, Victorian morality did not associate itself exclusively with any segment of Christianity; in fact, it had been remarkably secularized. For the overwhelming majority of Victorians who associated themselves with formal religion, moral standards suffused the churches, rather than vice versa. One finds the sources of Victorian morality outside, not inside, the churches, though one still learns much about Victorians by looking at the churches.

The "religious census" of 1851 best provides some useful facts about London's churches during Dickens' lifetime.

Church or Sect	Number of Churches	Seating For
Church of England	458	410,000
Independent (Congregationalists)	161	100,500
Baptists (five groups)	130	54,000
Methodists (four connections)	124	48,000
Roman Catholic	35	18,230
Presbyterians (two groups)	18	14,000
Church of Scotland	5	4,000
Jewish	11	3,700
Foreign Churches or Chapels	13	3,500
Quakers	9	3,300
Mormons	20	2,700
Moravians	2	1,100
All Others	102	23,000

The upper and middle classes utterly dominated the churches and largely (wholly in most cases) provided the attendance. The census showed that the nonconformists (all denominations except the Church of England, Church of Scotland, and foreign chapels) used their buildings much more fully than the Anglicans, and the Anglicans also had the disadvantage of so many churches concentrated in areas of declining population (the City, districts near the City boundaries, Holborn, old Westminster).

Between 1851 and 1870 a good deal of new church building was set in motion, especially by the Anglicans and Congregationalists. The Established Church began vigorously building new churches as early as 1822. Both Anglicans and Congregationalists built churches and chapels in the new suburbs; both engaged in a very considerable redistribution of their resources within the metropolis. The Established Church moved south, west, and north from the older built-up areas to do new work; the nonconformist Protestants went east, south, and west. The Congregationalists began their great push to reach the lower classes; by the end of the century anyone could recognize the utter failure of the attempt. Congregationalists espoused an unqualifiedly middle-class Christianity, as did other sects. The Established Church, on the other hand, more than held its own in the appeal to the middle classes and, in the long run, was virtually the only Protestant church appealing to any portion of the working classes. In London, too, men who thought of themselves as among the elite tended to become Anglican even more quickly than in the provinces.

The Church of England had in London the more famous symbols of its history and its present work. St. Paul's Cathedral, the diocesan seat of the bishop of London, towered over the City and was Wren's world-famous symbol for the metropolis itself. Westminster Abbey, somewhat overshadowed by the new Houses of Parliament, already had its floors, walls, and corners filled with tombs of and monuments to the famous. Across the river in Lambeth the archbishop of Canterbury kept his London palace. Dozens of famous churches marked the metropolis: Wren's in and near the City, Hawksmoor's and other eighteenth-century monuments to the social prestige of the Church.

Roman Catholics also made London their center. In 1850, the Pope set off new cries of "No Popery!" in Britain by creating an English episcopal hierarchy. The primate of England was to be called the "archbishop of Westminster"; Anglicans set up a cry about "the papal aggression." Cardinal Wiseman became the first archbishop in 1850 and lived until 1865. Cardinal Manning succeeded him. Manning more than any other single Catholic made Roman Catholicism tolerably respectable in Britain. Manning had converted to Catholicism yet managed to preserve some of his high social and political associations. The steady trickle of English converts drew attention to the Catholic Church and helped to soften the English prejudice against the "Irish" and "foreign" Church somewhat. Before Newman's conversion in 1845, the Church had been largely composed of a few English aristocrats, their dependents, a few intellectuals, and the great mass of Irish immigrants into London, Liverpool, Chester, and Manchester. Irish Catholics always far outnumbered English Catholics in England itself, and since Irishmen used their religious faith as a weapon against English domination of Ireland, the Roman Catholic in England lived under perpetual strain.

For the Anglicans and Roman Catholics, at least, the metropolis served as their national center. The Anglican primate might have his seat in Canterbury, but since the Church of England was a national church, the government in Westminster utterly controlled it. Archbishops and bishops sat in the House of Lords but had relatively little to say about the administrative reforms imposed on the Church by the governments of the late 1830's, 1840's, and 1850's. The Roman Catholics in the title of their primate acknowledged the importance of London. Also, A. W. Pugin, the converted Catholic who largely provided the decorative symbolism of the new Houses of Parliament (where, ironically, the ultimate authority over the Church of England resided), contributed much to the building and decoration of new Catholic churches throughout London. Besides Anglicans and Catholics, Wesleyan Methodists considered some sort of London headquarters before 1870 but did not actually establish such headquarters for another generation.

In the religious life of London one cannot draw a firm line to separate actual nondenominational religious services and moral lectures; both were important during the century. Moral lectures were largely sermons without any pretense of a religious service, and they shaded into secular sermons about self-improvement. Exeter Hall in the Strand particularly served as a site for Sunday services and weekday lectures for evangelicals. Organizers of such affairs used any respectable building (temperance music halls would do) in the metropolis.

Just toward the end of Dickens' life a new evangelical spirit spread among the British middle and artisan classes. The "second evangelical revival," as some have called it, was a pale, weak reflection of the first such wave of religious enthusiasm in the late eighteenth century. There was a new surge of hymn-writing, and a certain increase in these nondenominational services and lectures. American-style revivalism even showed itself, particularly in the person of Dwight Moody. Moody, an American, rented Her Majesty's Theatre. The new ripple set off a nonconformist determination to reach out to the working masses and to surpass the Anglicans. They made their major effort in London, however, after 1870.

If nineteenth century Britain's theater and music leave one unimpressed, her literature is a staggering contrast. Even to attempt a short description of London's role is misleading. The incredible richness of experience and literary creativity has inspired endless volumes, not so much on London itself as on the scores of brilliant and creditable writers who lived in the metropolis during the first seven decades of the century.

London casts a giant shadow across the whole of cultured society. As with virtually every other facet of British life in the century, one can find vitality and national influence in the provinces, but London as a contrast or comparison is omnipresent. One can actually manage more easily an adequate description of those writers who did *not* live and work in London, but that would have no purpose.

London's publishing houses, society, and diversity attracted writers and all intellectuals to it. Here they could form cliques as they might choose. The landed classes (peerage and gentry) dominated county society; the business elites of Manchester, Birmingham, Leeds, and an increasing number of other towns dominated social and cultural life in the industrial centers. Provincial society might indeed inspire a writer, but only in London could there be a continuing, vigorous social and intellectual life which centered on the writers themselves. In London, the brilliant aristocrats or businessmen became the addenda of the writers' society, rather than the reverse.

London was too large and diverse to be cozily restrictive, like Paris and New York. The metropolis did not foster urban parochialism, though undoubtedly London had its share of such parochial minds. Without utterly draining the remainder of the nation of its talent and cultural initiative, London provided a convenient, exciting, rich locale for work and talk. It also provided means of support other than writing, which was not especially lucrative in his own time except for Dickens himself.

Some of the greatest writers of the century had virtually nothing to do directly with London, except to be published there. Jane Austen, George Crabbe, Sir Walter Scott, Wordsworth, the Brontës, Charles Darwin, Edward Fitzgerald, and Elizabeth Gaskell are usually associated with other parts of the nation rather than the metropolis. London still provided them with the necessary services to communicate their creativity to the society. Other writers had casual contact with London or followed professional inclination elsewhere while still sharing in the literary life of the metropolis. Byron, Shelley, De Quincey, Matthew Arnold, Charles Kingsley, Tennyson, and Trollope might be considered among these. For them, London played no especially vital part in their creativity, yet it was essential to their contact with the literate public.

Other writers came to London late, to settle down somewhat, to influence, and even to die. Samuel Taylor Coleridge in his forties came to Highgate in 1816, his creativity spent, and remained until his death in 1834. London's intellectuals could come *up* to him there, as Carlyle both sarcastically and admiringly pointed out. William Godwin, who died in 1836, also settled in London to live a somewhat quieter life—or at least a less restless one.

One cannot imagine some writers and intellectuals out of the metropolitan setting. William Blake was essentially a London man, dying there in 1827. His tragic, lonely brilliance transcends the life of the city. Still, as virtually every writer on London has at least mentioned, such a large city can provide more privacy, and more utter isolation, than any other single environment. Blake saw the potential and the horror of the urban life around him, even though he does not always seem to have been a part of it.

Jeremy Bentham was born in London, and in his association with London University and the *Westminster Review* he seems irrevocably an intimate part of London life. His utilitarian and mock-utilitarian followers likewise fixed on London as their intellectual center, even though Manchester seized the initiative as the political and economic center of Benthamite ideas. James Mill not only defined some of Bentham's concepts for a larger public but also applied the cold logic of utilitarianism to Indian government while he worked as a major administrative official in the East India Company. His son, John Stuart Mill, can hardly be imagined outside London. J. S. Mill's career focused on the intellectual *salon*, the diverse ideas to be assimilated into his developing philosophy, the East India Company (where he too reached the height of the administrative structure), and the politics of the capital. From 1865 to 1868 he was even M. P. for Westminster. Mill seems ideally the intellectual suited only to the metropolis: too abstract, too sophisticated, too intellectually remote for any other existence.

Carlyle, in so many ways a vividly intense Scot, lived in London from 1834 until his death in 1881. Carlyle became the Isaiah of his age, even developing a prophetic style of prose to complete his pose. He predicted doom for the society around him and still offered tiny, significant specks of hope. At one time a friend of John Stuart Mill, and for many years a friend of Dickens, he was lionized by anyone in London with the slightest intellectual pretense, and he left an unforgettable impression on his contemporaries. Mill's vague manner obscured for those who talked with him his comprehensively brilliant mind; Carlyle's manner and presence gave promise of an intellectual depth which his written work never achieved. He obviously thrived in London, where for the first time he had scope for his psychotic, intellectualized rage. Carlyle hated the noise and crowd of London. He slashed at the materialistic world around him as if London were the original Babylon. Yet he had a compulsive need for an audience. He was a man with the hermit's or ascetic's manner who displayed it in the cultivated literary *salons* of the world's greatest city. It was not the least of Carlyle's many contradictions and poses.

Thomas Campbell, another Scot and a poet who came permanently to London just after the turn of the century, contributed time and energy and perhaps even the original idea to the establishment of University College. Thomas Love Peacock, a highly sophisticated novelist, worked for the East India Company as an administrative official. Walter Bagehot, with some impressive but not brilliant literary essays to his name, became editor of the *Economist* and wrote practical surveys of the political and economic world he knew (*The English Constitution* and *Lombard Street*). Bulwer Lytton cultivated a real if second-rank talent for fiction, an interest in politics, and dilettantism. London was perfect for all three.

Thackeray, Wilkie Collins, Charles Reade, and George Meredith all lived in London. Thackeray in particular wrote about the life he saw around him. Several of his novels, such as *Pendennis* and *The Newcomes*, are as full of London life though not as full of Londoners as any of Dickens' novels. Thackeray also associated himself closely with the literary periodical press, contributing to *Punch* and editing the *Cornhill*. Charles Lamb's literary friendships, perhaps as inconsequential as his writing, nevertheless brought many writers together in London in the first third of the century. (Lamb, not so incidentally, was another employee of the East India Company.) Hazlitt, Southey, Robert Browning (except for his fifteen years of marriage and life in Italy), John Ruskin, Herbert Spencer (once a subeditor of the *Economist*), and Leslie Stephen largely remained in London during their productive years.

Among these writers, and also among the editors, journalists, artists, intellectuals, and pseudo intellectuals who abounded in the metropolis, significant friendships and associations gave London an especially appealing world of letters. As a professional class, intellectuals gained increased confidence. Minor dynasties of literati even established themselves within the ranks. Sir James Stephen, one of the earliest professional civil servants of high governmental rank, was father of Sir James Fitzjames Stephen and Leslie Stephen. The former wrote famous works on jurisprudence; the latter married Thackeray's daughter and worked his way into Thackeray's influential position among literary periodicals. Leslie Stephen's wife died without children, and he remarried. His two daughters from the second marriage were Virginia Woolf and Vanessa Bell; the Woolf family was the hard core of the "Bloomsbury Circle" of the 1920's, a logical and infinitely self-conscious intellectual development out of the literary world of Victorian London.

Another succession was that of Lord Macaulay (historian, essayist, politician, editor of the *Edinburgh Review*), Sir George Otto Trevelyan (Macaulay's brother-in-law, cabinet minister, popular historian), and George Macaulay Trevelyan (Macaulay's nephew, the heir of his library, a great and popular historian). The Huxleys and the Stracheys also supplied professional intellectuals for more than one generation.

Most of these men and women, admittedly, built the great substructure of intellectual life; the greatest names of the era stand more alone. Dickens had innumerable friendships; in fact, he seemed to know every writer worth any attention at all during his lifetime. He cultivated Thackeray, Carlyle, Wilkie Collins, and Bulwer Lytton as more special friends and courted scores of others for at least their easy acquaintance. Dickens undoubtedly fit all of these pieces into the mosaic of his art, yet he was so compulsive about his friendships that one calculates them as emotional and not intellectual affiliations. Likewise, he borrowed characters from the newspapers, from his observations of London, and from Henry Mayhew's *London Labour and the London Poor*. It was all a great, wild whirl of literary genius, and a genius of which the depths of meaning are only now being discovered a century after his death.

Trollope, in contrast to Dickens, remained aloof from London and literary society. George Eliot did not participate so energetically but was probably more receptive to significant ideas than either Mill or Ruskin, who did circulate. All of this activity widened and deepened the self-conscious, skillful, derivative levels of intellectual life. Creative genius did not rely upon such a life, but it had more to work with because of it. London provided the locale in which so many writers and men of letters could make a living. They could also sense more quickly and deeply their own importance; they saw their place in the society which was British, and then European. Writers need not apologize in London for their existence. If no one else wished to listen to them, they could talk to each other. Again, we return to the potential danger of a literary world too isolated from the rest of its society. London's literary world, however, spoke to the whole society through rapidly expanding levels of publication.

No publisher of any real consequence existed outside London and Edinburgh, and the Scottish capital lost ground in every way to London during the first third of the nineteenth century. The publishers Constable and Blackwood reflected glory on Edinburgh; in 1826 Constable went bankrupt, ironically enough, because of the failure of his London agents.

London's publishers steadily extended their dominance in the second and third quarters of the century. John Murray, a Scot who settled in London, published Byron, Scott, Coleridge, Southey, Lockhart, Crabbe, Jane Austen, and Leigh Hunt. He also published the *Quarterly Review*. Taylor and Hessey (who published Hazlitt, De Quincey, Lamb, and the *London Magazine*), Henry Colburn (Bulwer Lytton and other novelists), Longman's of Paternoster Row, Chapman and Hall (Dickens), and Bradbury and Evans (Dickens after 1844) were other great names in London publishing.

Publishers supplied patronage to authors in the nineteenth century, replacing the enlightened aristocrats of the eighteenth century. Payments for creative work crept upward. Until 1830 the public bought poetry; after 1830 it supported fiction to a much greater extent. Consequently, publishers' cash payments naturally followed the trend of general interests. All books were exceedingly costly until 1850, and only gradually did authors, publishers, and booksellers begin to cater to a mass public.

Scott had exposed the gold-bearing strata of popular fiction, but Dickens mined it. He tapped the magazine serial, the cheap hard-bound complete edition, and the lush "library" edition. His relationships with his two greatest publishers were lucrative for all concerned, but in both cases a blowup resulted. Virtually every author despised or pretended to despise his publisher, believing him a charlatan, thief, and blackmailer. But few could demand of their publishers what Dickens could demand, and get it. Dickens sensed the mood of his public and incorporated this perception into the very life of his novels. Romantics and idealists about literature have never been able to accept such a rapport with one's public as compatible with art and have consequently doubted Dickens' art. Such judgment is ridiculous and ignores the ability of the man to make creative use of virtually anything which he saw, read, heard, or touched.

The public taste in books in the period from 1816 to 1851 is best illustrated by some statistics derived from Charles Knight on the number of titles published in certain categories.

Theology, sermons, religion	10,300
History and geography	4,900

Foreign languages and school books	4,000
Fiction	3,500
Drama and poetry	3,400
Juvenile books	2,900
Medical	2,500
Arts	2,460
Science	2,450
Industry, economics, statistics	2,350
Biography	1,850
Law	1,850
Morals, moral instruction, guidance	1,400
Other	1,400

But in total volumes published, fiction became king.

From the 1820's the new phenomenon of cheap-edition publishing struck the publishing world. The older publishers resisted the onslaught but slowly gave way to lower prices and mass circulation. Trash fiction, political pamphlets, speeches, moral tales, doggerel poetry, songs—the variety and quantity seemed, and seems, infinite. In the long run, however, books were no longer for the elite and the circulating libraries alone. The era of popular culture was just beginning, with all its opportunities.

Dickens' London also opened up a broad new level of periodical publication in conjunction with these trends. Quarterly reviews, monthlies, fortnightlies, weekly journals and magazines, weekly reviews and newspapers tumbled over one another throughout the century. Political, intellectual, and literary coteries established organs to convince all other men (and themselves, too, for that matter) of "Truth": their truth, of course. Polemics required readers. All groups eventually returned to education as the answer to Britain's problems—or rather, the vehicle for reaching the final answers. Education became the common denominator of all Victorian theories, principles, and systems, just as religious faith had been the common denominator of medieval systems and theories. The very confusion of persuasions underlined Britain's, and London's, vigor.

In 1855, the compulsory newspaper stamp tax was abolished, opening up the whole of the periodical press for inexpensive, and often cheap, popular journalism. Many periodicals had not been subject to the tax, but the elimination of it gave impetus to the growth of the whole periodical press. Technological innovation, first with newspapers, influenced all publications. The steam-driven press, the rotary press, the telegraph and cable for quick information, and the railroad for rapid distribution made enormous difference to the whole of the press.

For a particularly rapid expansion of popular culture based upon the printed word, another component was absolutely necessary: a willing, literate public which bought, and hopefully read, what was produced. More and more Britons achieved literacy during the century. In 1812, perhaps three-quarters of all Englishmen were illiterate; Scotland's proportion of illiterate may have been slightly lower, and Ireland's was much, much higher. In 1870, in contrast, only twenty per cent of all Englishmen were illiterate. The Established Church, the dissenters, boroughs, and philanthropists had established schools; the government and the public even acknowledged the necessity of broadly conceived, enforced standards. They had unwittingly accepted a first principle of the welfare state, inspection. Then, with the Education Act of 1870, Great Britain had the makings of a universal (but not free) elementary education system.

Dickens' lifetime corresponds almost exactly with the years during which the great quarterly reviews held forth, even though his association with them was negligible. Quarterly reviews did not encourage mass culture. They appealed to the elite; publishers supported them as attractions for the book trade. All of the quarterlies published review articles of significant books, but authors frequently used the review technique as a mere excuse for a literary or political essay of significant proportions. Mill and Macaulay published their greatest essays in quarterly reviews, for instance. Both were at one time editors, Mill of the *Westminster Review* and Macaulay of the *Edinburgh Review*.

The *Edinburgh Review* was established first in 1803. That Macaulay moved the editing of it to London emphasized the decline of Edinburgh as a chief cultural center, which it had been in the late eighteenth and early nineteenth centuries. The *Edinburgh* was Whig—enlightened Whig, but still Whig. In the 1860's it circulated about 7,000 copies of each issue. The *Quarterly Review* was the foremost publication of this type from the moment it was established in 1809. Its sympathies were decidedly Tory—enlightened Tory, but still Tory. Published in London by John Murray, in over-all commentary it surpassed all of its major rivals, though the others had their great names such as Mill and Macaulay.

In 1824, the Benthamite Radicals created the *Westminster Review*, where Bentham, the Mills, George Grote, Sir John Bowring, and a host of the new radical breed could strike at what they considered Tory and Whig nonsense alike. The radicals made their organ the vehicle for their ideas about progress, free trade, reform, peace, and retrenchment (i.e., economy in government). They assumed a consistency in their philosophy which could comprehend literature as well. As in no other periodical, men dedicated to a new urbanized, industrialized, democratized society tried to apply their sympathies to every facet of British life. In 1865, another radical periodical, the *Fortnightly Review*, dedicated itself to the newly formed Liberal Party; a year later Liberals with a greater interest in evangelical Protestantism established the *Contemporary Review*.

These dedicated yet judicious and relatively contemplative publications encouraged others. Without cataloguing the scores of publications which were published in London, it can be stated that a few which Dickens knew survive still. The *Economist*, especially under Walter Bagehot, achieved status among politically and economically minded readers. The *Spectator*, like most others, combined literature and politics. One of the most effective publications was the Tory *Saturday Review*, which featured particularly fine writing in its first few decades after 1855.

In monthly magazines, Thackeray's *Cornhill* began very strongly in 1860 with a circulation of 80,000, but this rapidly dropped. All other London monthlies together circulated in the 1860's about 50,000 copies each month. For weeklies, *Punch* began in 1841, and the *Illustrated London News* in 1842. Weeklies ranged from popular literature (Dickens' *All the Year Round*) to near trash (*London Journal*). All London weeklies together probably sold about 1,275,000 copies throughout the nation each week during 1870.

Among the newspapers of the era, only the *Times* could claim to be an undoubted institution of influence, responsibility, stuffiness, and egomania. The *Times* believed profoundly in its own legend—probably an absolute necessity for any publication. Few of the world's newspapers have ever matched the *Times* for its position in national affairs, and no newspaper can boast such a long dominance. Though frankly Tory and High Anglican in sentiments, the *Times* frequently published the views of other parties. The Walters, owners of the newspaper, constantly experimented with publication devices, if with little else. They first used the steam press and contributed importantly to the development of the rotary press. Before 1830 the newspaper was issuing the predecessors of its now famous "supplements." It worked carefully to produce accurate accounts of speeches in Parliament, always featuring an important account of parliamentary intelligence. Its foreign department frequently had quicker and more detailed news from overseas than the Foreign Office, but then, the same might be said of the *New York Times* as against the United States Department of State in our own time. The *Times* slowly and reluctantly accepted the use of professional wire-service news, mainly because it had such superb services of its own correspondents; but after the mid-1850's Reuter and then others sold services to the *Times*. As a prime example of its egomania, the newspaper at first paid Reuter double for his news in order not to have to acknowledge in print where it had obtained the news.

Particularly during the editorship of John Thadeus Delane (1841–78) the *Times* combined its "thundering" traditions (satirized by Trollope in *The Warden*) with incredibly impressive intelligence operations at home and abroad. Delane was one of the greatest editors in the history of journalism. He did not himself usually write for his newspaper, instead cultivating the friendships and associations which would guarantee him the most intimate knowledge of happenings within government offices and even the

Cabinet itself. Prime ministers bitterly resented the knowledge which the newspaper possessed; Lord Aberdeen and Lord John Russll both protested the tyranny of the *Times*. Such journalism may have kept governments honest and relatively straightforward. Who was to do the same with the *Times*?

The newspaper also had its uses for the government. It became in effect the semiofficial organ, testing public opinion with the calculated "leak." Delane still maintained the newspaper's independence, maintaining at any moment his connections within both the government and the opposition. He was, then, virtually a shadow member of every government and opposition group. Printing House Square, the home of the *Times*, stood for a new type of power, and for many it suggested dangerous power: the "fourth estate," independent of the other three. Dangerous because it was responsible to no one in any traditional sense. Such an institution was not trusted by English politicians. Only when several newspapers as powerful and as continuous as the *Times* could serve the public by representing different views would some sort of balance resembling that of the quarterly reviews be achieved. No such newspapers developed before 1870.

Rivals to the *Times* made little impact. The *Standard*, established in 1827, was still Tory, offering no real alternative. The *Daily News* began in 1846 with a disastrous editorship of none other than Charles Dickens. Journalist he was; editor he was not. The Liberal-to-Radical *News* survived, but as a more or less stagnant journal. The Liberal *Daily Telegraph* began in 1855, piously and inexpensively to repeat incantations about progress, improvement, free trade, individualism, economy in government, reform, etc.

After 1870 the newspaper improved its own style and tone and became a far more formidable rival to the *Times*. It had twice the circulation of Delane's newspaper, or about 150,000. One evening paper, the *Echo*, appeared first in 1868 with a Liberal editorial policy. It quickly matched the *Times*' circulation but had very limited influence, if any at all. Evening newspapers had their era much later.

Weekly newspapers of all varieties had a circulation of 1,000,000 in 1870; half of that was held by *Lloyd's Weekly* alone. With *Lloyd's*, *Reynold's Weekly*, and *News of the World*, the scarcely educated lower middle classes (mainly shopkeepers and office clerks and artisans) found their media.

From trash to highly intellectualized trivia, from high society to religious pretention, from impassioned politics to fashions, publications of every variety poured their offerings before Victoria's literate and semiliterate subjects. In London the total publication figures by 1870 were approximately:

Daily Newspapers	450,000
Weekly Newspapers	1,200,000
Weekly Reviews	75,000
Other Reviews (literary, scientific, religious)	55,000
Magazines	1,100,000

Certainly no single city in the world could match such emissions, for better or for worse.

One would be hard pressed to prove that formal education had much to do directly with this realm of the printed word, but a discussion of the one provokes thoughts about the other. London's pattern followed that of most of England: a confusion of charity schools, private academies, endowed institutions, and religious establishments. A brief summary of all registered schools in the metropolis in the 1860's would be:

Type	Number	Students
1. Public Day Schools including:	860	167,000
Endowed Collegiate and Grammar	19	3,800
Other Endowed	80	12,300
Church of England	375	80,000
Congregational	64	11,000
Roman Catholic	42	7,800
Other Denominational	38	9,000
Workhouse	26	4,000
Orphan	18	2,000
Ragged	74	15,500
2. Private Day Schools	3,700	87,000
3. Sunday Schools including:	700	140,000
Church of England	250	49,000
Congregationalist	156	39,000
4. Evening Schools (Adult)	100	3,000

The variation in quality and type represented in these statistics virtually renders the whole incomprehensible. The best among the collegiate and grammar schools were St. Pauls' in the cathedral churchyard (removed in the 1880's to Hammersmith), Charterhouse (transferred to Godalming, Surrey, in 1872), and King's College School. At the opposite end of the scale many endowed and private schools barely taught literacy to their students. The Sunday Schools tried to teach a little reading and writing to working-class children.

What is surprising is how much was accomplished in the chaos of institutions below the best; literacy did increase, as we have seen. Good education was still very much for the respectable elite, with some liberalization just noticeable.

When dissenting Protestants, radicals, and rationalists established London University in 1836, they increased the impetus of educational change. The quiet reformers at Oxford and Cambridge, still few in number, pushed the ancient universities out of their eighteenth-century lethargy before the Reform Bill, but both of them (Oxford more so) were still tightly controlled corporations suspicious of extraordinary (non-Anglican) students. By obtaining a university, and London was the last major European capital to do so, the metropolis gained a genuinely important nucleus for educational progress. It did not rival Oxford and Cambridge until the twentieth century, but it was genuinely an institution of higher learning much earlier than that.

Henry Brougham, Thomas Campbell the poet, and other Radical Whigs established "London University" in 1826 on Gower Street. When the government chartered London University in 1836, the proprietors of the Gower Street institution changed its name to University College and received a charter. With Faculties of Arts and Laws, Science, and Medicine, and a department of civil and mechanical engineering, the proprietary institution was meant to be a center of liberal, scientific, and progressive (i.e., "modern") views. The complex proprietary rights confused University

College affairs until 1869, when the government settled all issues which had not been negotiated. By this time, University College had a library of 68,000 volumes and 18,000 pamphlets. What is more, it had the best science laboratories in England.

The government chartered London University in 1836 as an examining institution only; University College was one of its two most important affiliates. In its first year the university examined thirty-three candidates for degrees. By 1870 it examined about 1,500 candidates annually. The university came to be housed in this era in Pennethorne's impressive Palladian building on the south side of Burlington Gardens. No one can be as self-conscious about architectural monuments as academics or those associated with academia. They imagine that their importance in society demands a monument which has both immediate and lasting cultural meaning. They are right. The commissioners negotiating the university's new quarters first had to decide upon the style of the building, but this was a simple process compared to the agonizing decisions concerning the statuary which would decorate the new building. The figures must be representative of intellectual tradition. In the long run the commissioners chose Sir Isaac Newton to represent the Faculty of Science, Jeremy Bentham to represent the Faculty of Law, John Milton the Faculty of Arts (Shakespeare was rejected for being exceedingly nonacademic), and William Harvey the Faculty of Medicine. Three groups of intellectual greats represented the Ancients, the Continentals, and the British (a rather revealing grouping in itself). The Ancients selected were Galen, Aristotle, Plato, Archimedes, Cicero, and Justinian. The Continentals were Galileo, Goethe, Laplace, Leibnitz, Cuvier, and Linnaeus. The British were Hunter (?!), Hume, Davy, Adam Smith, Locke, and Bacon.

King's College, intensely Anglican and a deliberate counter to "that Godless institution" University College, made up the other major college affiliated before 1870 to the University, besides University College itself. The Crown chartered King's in 1828. The government housed the college in Smirke's wing of Somerset House, where higher education, evening classes, and the school all existed as a part of the institution (remarkably like most American institutions). King's had Faculties of Theology, General Literature and Science, Applied Sciences, and Medicine.

Other institutions which later became colleges affiliated to the University originated in the early and middle nineteenth century. Birkbeck Literary and Scientific Institution was established in 1823; Bedford College for women located itself initially in 1849 in Bedford Square. The Christian Socialists' Working Men's College was vaguely affiliated to the University in 1856, two years after Frederick Maurice and John Malcolm Ludlow inspired its establishment. In 1872 Thomas Hughes, author of *Tom Brown's School Days*, became principal; the college was incorporated in 1876.

In scientific education and experimental science the British Institution (established in 1799) added importantly to the early, rather feeble efforts of the university. The British Institution gave facilities to Davy and Farraday, among others.

Another important aspect of public education during the century was the persistent vogue for lecturing. Coleridge, Hazlitt, and Carlyle were among the greatest lecturers of

the era, but virtually any figure of any note in any vocation
had one try at lecturing. Not only did men of learning gain
further income from such efforts; the public also satiated
some of its hunger for knowledge. The *bourgeoisie* thought
it needed "self-improvement"; learning could be acquired
like daily pennies and put into the savings bank of the
mind. No political or pressure campaign after 1830 could
be complete without its traveling lecturers. With its own
special ritual, the lecture was the secularized sermon. The
dissenting *bourgeoisie* took their religion in pious but
modest bites, choosing passively to receive theology by
way of the sermon. The lecture served the same secular
purpose. Dickens catered to the lecturing impulses of his
public but added to his readings more than a mere touch of
the theater. Entertainment replaced enlightenment in his
performances.

London's cultural life ranged from simple to elaborate
pleasure, from the mere passing of time to the creation of
ideas which gave purpose to an empire. In some of its
activities, London acted without particular relevance to the
rest of British society. Londoners enjoyed or improved
themselves in ways unique to them and largely unrelated to
others, just as did the inhabitants of Birmingham, or Manchester, or Edinburgh. Such activities and interests drew
more and steadier attention because of the size of London
and because so many foreigners and Britons visited London.

And, like any other city, London also engaged in some
activities not at all trivial which deeply influenced other
Britons. Essentially, much of the point of this book is that
London did so much of importance in these categories that
her influence penetrated more deeply than other urban

centers, and perhaps all of them combined. As the only British urban center deserving of the name "metropolis," London absorbed the raw stuff of civilization from the whole of the nation, and from Europe and the remainder of the world beyond.

Britain's elite made London the brain-center of its civilization. By responding to impulses from Manchester, or Scotland, or India, or Capetown—or, for that matter, by *failing* to respond to impulses from Ireland or Germany—the elite formed many of the ideas and ideals for the whole of British society.

When Dickens was born, only the first stirrings of a new civilization touched London. When he died, industrialization, urbanization, expansion overseas, and political democracy had deeply moved Great Britain. London became even more than before the center of this civilization. Changes had not made British society democratic. Whatever the appearances in politics, the reins of power remained in the hands of the elite.

The elite which London housed had been expanded by 1870. It looked with new tolerance on money and talent as prime endorsements for membership. A few among the elite of 1870 worried about the undemocratic nature of the whole society. A few thought cultural democracy as important as political democracy. Largely, however, the elite thought with Matthew Arnold that mass culture was no culture at all, and that the very few deserving and responsible leaders refined, defined, and promulgated the all-inclusive cultural laws. John Stuart Mill's ambiguous defense of democracy was hardly a defense at all. Liberals could only suggest education of all men as a real alternative to traditional society, and even they recognized the utopian absurdity of such a suggestion in their own time. "Everything, and nothing, changes"—from the pinnacle of London's elite culture, so it seemed.

London's aristocrats and intellectuals did not make the metropolis a citadel of culture against a lumpish, alien hinterland. One might describe nineteenth-century Vienna, Boston, or perhaps even Paris in these terms, though in the latter case Paris so drained France of cultural initiative that no other alternative seemed possible. England was not a lumpish, alien hinterland to London. London had no rival British city in art, music, belles-lettres, and similar cultural activities, but in economics and politics she had articulate challengers. After 1870 Birmingham offered as national alternatives tariff protection, imperial expansion, and the raw vigor of aggressive business rivalry with new economic powers on the continent of Europe and in America. London could not afford to be and was not a citadel of culture, nor was she self-satisfied and remote from these challenges behind an impregnable wall of proven superiority.

Instead, London's sophistication and eclecticism linked Britain with Europe and the world, and in a manner which weakened the independence of the nation-state. In the imperfect nineteenth-century world of resurgent nation-states and interhemispheric rivalries leading to catastrophic war in the twentieth century, London's cultural achievements had a touch of tragedy about them. The metropolis exposed itself, and the nation-empire of which it was capital, to the buffetings of a viciously competitive era. At the same time, her nineteenth-century interests—cultural, economic, and political—may prove to be prophetic of the new and broader associations of late twentieth-century Britain.

Already by 1870 London gave the impression, false perhaps, that she could have stood alone as a metropolis, without England if need be. Culturally as well as economically,
London had become the world town.

V

... *And Enormous Pain*

LONDON, following Leigh Hunt's equation, had its experience of enormous pain as well as its quantity of pleasure. Any urban center presented new difficulties to Britain's rulers, who were inexperienced and unsophisticated about urban problems, though no more so than any other national leaders. Manchester, or Preston, or Bolton, or Rochdale—Dickens' "Coketown" in *Hard Times*—seemed brutally simple, however, as compared to London. Industrialization in the northern and midland towns abruptly scarred the landscape, built new towns, boomed old towns, and brought working men, women, and children into factories and mines. If landed aristocrats could criticize such conditions as unnatural, the factory owners could likewise point an accusing finger at the undeveloped, nearly primitive countryside. London, obviously, was neither one nor the other; it was a law unto itself, outside the more obvious social-political-economic conflicts of the century. London baffled reformers—at least those thinking in terms of general reform.

In the great decades of "High Victorian" prosperity (the 1850's, 1860's, and 1870's) poverty nevertheless kept its grip on many rural and urban Britons. How many Londoners lived below the line of poverty in 1870? Following some of the most pessimistic commentators of the century, perhaps as many as 1,000,000 Londoners lived a good portion of their lives without sufficient housing, clothing, or food. In other words, not quite one-third of the metropolitan population suffered poverty on occasion. A much smaller proportion suffered unrelieved, continuous poverty.

Some pieces of information here and there would indicate that the estimate of 1,000,000 may not be outrageously exaggerated. In 1867, over 100,000 Londoners received poor relief from the official rates, and under the harsh conditions which the Poor Law of 1834 established. Economically, that year experienced some revival after the financial panic of 1866. The relatively light depression hit trade, and therefore the ports, harder than industry. London's dockers were terribly vulnerable to economic fluctuations, and the "recession" of 1866–67 took its toll among them. Another 150,000 Londoners may in 1867 have received private relief from charitable institutions. With such estimates as these, one can well imagine another 750,000 having insufficient food, shelter, or clothing.

"High Victorian" prosperity trickled down to the lower classes slowly, though real wages certainly did go up after 1850. The repeal of the Corn Laws and an efficient British agriculture drove food prices down, but London's poor remained vulnerable to widespread adulteration of both food and drugs. Angry reformers in the 1860's, agitating for the reform of Parliament, played a subtheme about food adulteration. Sawdust in the flour was a frequent trick. Not until 1875 did a Tory government (Disraeli's) pass a modest pure food and drug act.

General prosperity did little for working-class housing in London. Whitechapel, Bethnal Green, South Holborn, and

Westminster had filthy, horrible slums, but near-slum housing spread through most of the metropolis. Philanthropists
built experimental dwellings in parts of London and dabbled with slum clearance and model tenements. The central
authority did nothing until Disraeli's government encouraged modest slum clearance with a statute passed in
1875. Such efforts fell pathetically short of need. Liberals,
paralyzed by a highly developed suspicion of the state, left
the initiative to the Tories. Actually, the administrative
structure of the state was still too crude to function ade-
quately in broad welfare matters.

Dickens described one of the worst London "rookeries"
or slums, St. Giles' in Holborn, in *Bleak House* (ch. XVI).
Tom-all-Alone's is Jo the Crossing Sweeper's home:

> Jo lives—that is to say, Jo has not yet died—in a ruinous
> place, known to the like of him by the name of Tom-
> all-Alone's. It is a black, dilapidated street, avoided by all
> decent people; where the crazy houses were seized upon,
> when their decay was far advanced, by some bold
> vagrants, who, after establishing their own possession,
> took to letting them out in lodgings. Now, these tumb-
> ling tenements contain, by night, a swarm of misery. As,
> on the ruined human wretch, vermin parasites appear, so
> these ruined shelters have bred a crowd of foul existence
> that crawls in and out of gaps in walls and boards; and
> coils itself to sleep, in maggot numbers, where the rain
> drips in; and comes and goes, fetching and carrying fever,
> and sowing more evil in its every footprint than Lord
> Coodle, and Sir Thomas Doodle, and the Duke of Foodle,
> and all the fine gentlemen in office, down to Zoodle, shall
> set right in five hundred years—though born expressly to

do it. Twice, lately, there has been a crash and a cloud of dust, like the springing of a mine, in Tom-all-Alone's; and, each time, a house has fallen. These accidents have made a paragraph in the newspapers, and have filled a bed or two in the nearest hospital. The gaps remain, and there are not unpopular lodgings among the rubbish. As several more houses are nearly ready to go, the next crash in Tom-all-Alone's may be expected to be a good one.

The twelve worst "rookeries" housed probably between 200,000 and 225,000 Londoners. Scattered from Westminster to Stepney, and from Southwark to Holborn and Marylebone, they simply brought together all the worst possible conditions in London, intensifying the poverty, misery, filth, and crime. John Hollingshead in his *Ragged London in 1861* describes "rookeries" in Soho, St. James's, Westminster, St.-Martin's-in-the-Fields, Knightsbridge, Chelsea, Brentford, Lambeth, Walworth, Southwark, Somers' Town, Kentish Town, and Camden Town.

London's "rookeries" (the worst slums), of course, bred disease. Cause of death is frequently a meaningless phrase among the poor. Who knows the exact cause? One calculates instead the occasion of death. Of the more spectacular diseases of the century, cholera struck general fear. Ships from the Middle East generally brought cholera to the London docks, though occasionally the epidemics built up suspense by moving in slower stages through the Balkans, into Italy and southern France, and then to Britain. The last cholera epidemic in Dickens' lifetime hit London in 1866, taking nearly 4,000 lives. The inhabitants of Stepney and the rest of the East End suffered most, as one might expect.

The annual death rate in the metropolis in the late 1860's had dropped to about one in forty-nine. In 1815, it had been about one in thirty-eight, constantly improving until 1856. A ten-year period of increase then followed before the generally favorable trend renewed itself. On the whole, London's death rate compared favorably with the rest of Great Britain and was much more favorable than the rate in continental cities. Within the metropolis, rates differed enormously. In the 1860's the highest death rate persisted in Holborn, attesting to the particularly deadly slums which were finally rebuilt a full generation later. After Holborn, in order of declining death rate, stood the eastern parishes beyond the City, the northern parishes outside the City and Westminster, the southern parishes along the river, and finally the West End. Of course, the death rate reflected the concentrations of the poor. This grim ranking of areas apparently remained roughly the same during most of the years from 1800 to 1870, except that the southern parishes had a more sharply declining death rate after the introduction of better water supplies on south bank in the late 1850's.

The same miserable "rookeries" which bred disease harbored London's criminals. One must be suspicious of the so-called statistics about London crime; still, the information indicates the situation. One estimate gives 18,000 as the number of "hardened" criminals living by crime alone in the metropolis. Occasional breakers of the law would not be included. From among these 18,000 came the one-third of the prison population which was made up of multiple offenders who could be expected to commit further crimes.

Perhaps 30,000 regular petty thieves lived in London, supplementing their daily or occasional trades by such means. The Metropolitan Police believed that in the late

1860's some 1,500 professional receivers of stolen goods operated regularly in the metropolitan area. Stepney and Westminster sheltered more of these receivers and their "front" shops than other sections. Some 500 or more receivers lived in Westminster alone, the majority of them Irish. One could speculate that such receivers did considerable business with house servants, artisans, and the tradesmen who served the wealthy households of the West End. In the East End at Stepney the Jewish receivers probably did their business with dockers, warehousemen, petty river thieves, and others filching from or preying upon the traffic of the port.

Some 10,000 professional gamblers worked in London, which remained a center for the English mania of gambling. Moral earnestness had certainly quietened the Englishman's urge to bet or take chances, but enough gambling went on to be obvious even to rather unobserving visitors.

Deeply troubling to Englishmen was the knowledge that thousands of children trained to crime lived and operated in London. Dickens' *Oliver Twist* dramatized what was common knowledge. In the 1860's the relevant police information led some to believe that 20,000 such children were in London. They largely stole but also ran errands and kept up contacts for the criminals now being closely watched by the Metropolitan Police.

Interestingly enough, crimes of violence did not appear significantly among police statistics of the 1860's. Rape, murder, and assault found asylum in countryside, market town, city, or metropolis alike.

London, however, specialized in prostitution. The size of the metropolis, the port, the army, the hardened criminals, and high society encouraged the vice at one level or another. Estimated totals of prostitutes varied wildly. Many commentators tried their hand at estimating the total because London seemed so full of prostitutes. The police reported their knowledge of 8,000 regular prostitutes in the late 1860's. Based partially on this statistic, others guessed that some 20,000 prostitutes worked in the brothels or walked the streets. A few even believed that 80,000 women working regularly or occasionally as prostitutes lived in London. Prostitution shades into promiscuity; no one could define the exact limits of prostitution.

The vice touched all districts. Again, Stepney and Westminster had the dubious distinctions of probably supporting more prostitutes than other districts. The port and high society, respectively, provided the major business. From police reports in the nineteenth and twentieth centuries, not much has changed about the business. The fashionable "houses" of Westminster, the rather unpretentious brothels just off the Strand, the sordid brothels near the docks, the streetwalkers of the Haymarket (near the theaters and fashionable clubs), the common streetwalkers in any district, the "soldiers' prostitutes," and the "park women" (doing business in St. James's and Hyde Parks) marked the scope of prostitution. Considering how much the police in the 1860's did *not* know about London crime and vice, the larger estimate of 80,000 prostitutes looks reasonable.

Every social class provided the Victorians with their "fallen women," naturally. The servant class (there were 100,000 female household servants in London in 1870) provided the larger number, probably because such young girls went into household service and were so vulnerable to the men of the employer's family. Milliners, dressmakers, laundresses, seamstresses, and other artisan women took to prostitution in large numbers. Again, economic problems and working women's vulnerability to men of better class had influence. England's traditions of "deference" revealed themselves in varieties of ways, vice not excepted.

Foreigners, and especially continentals, remarked on London's vice. Parisians thought of London as a sinful city—a place where vice was more readily at hand than in any other European city. The diversity of vice apparently kept pace with the diversity of every other aspect of London.

Evangelical and bourgeois morality may well have made vice more sordid by driving it out of sight in Victoria's reign, rather than less prevalent, but Victorian moralists also supported an array of charities for relief and reform. Gladstone tried to reform individual prostitutes (a good Liberal approach): he did not concern himself deeply with the conditions which encouraged prostitution. Most of his contemporaries preferred a slightly less direct approach, having neither the courage nor the desire to pick up prostitutes on the street, as Gladstone did, and to buy their time in order to urge moral reform. The Society for the Rescue of Young Women and Children, London by Moonlight Mission, Society for the Suppression of Vice, London Society for the Protection of Young Females, Home of Hope, Reformatory and Refuge Union, Female Aid Society, Association for the Aid and Benefit of Dressmakers and Milliners, and Young Women's Christian Association and West End Home were but a few of the charitable agencies in London.

More than 550 charitable agencies in London alone dispensed aid in one form or another to the poor. Their accumulative income totaled nearly 2,000,000 pounds per year. One gazetteer published in the 1860's listed the charitable institutions as "general medical hospitals, lunatic asylums, special medical hospitals, residential hospitals, general dispensaries, alms-houses, refuges for the destitute, asylums for orphans, homes for the aged or the outcast, societies for relieving general distress and destitution, societies for relieving specific distress, societies for aiding cases of emergency or for preserving life, institutions for reforming offenders or reclaiming the fallen, societies for the ameliorating of public morals, societies for aiding the resources of the industrious, provident societies, charitable pension societies, religious book societies, Bible societies, missionary societies, and many institutions or associations of mixed or miscellaneous character."

Many Victorians of both the middle classes and aristocracy supported the charities, but the middle classes gave most of the funds which kept the asylums, refuges, societies, etc., functioning. Perhaps such philanthropists and casual givers deserve praise, but neither praise nor lack of it really have much to do with the condition of the poor and stricken. What is most striking about London's charities is that they in almost no way differed from charities throughout Christian history, except that, like most other things Victorian, charitable institutions had more tightly knit administrative structure. Beyond that, charities *relieved* the poor and stricken; they did nothing about the causes of the problems. In both the governmental and private approaches to social problems, social reformers gave a hint of concerns about causes. Yet in spite of a century and a half of the "Enlightenment" with its optimistic view of the nature of man, Victorians still viewed the poor and unfortunate as largely the causes of their own predicament. The ancient Christian doctrine of the essential depravity of man applied to the poor and unfortunate; enlightened, rationalist, optimistic "Liberalism" (the Victorian phase of the Enlightenment) applied to the prosperous.

Evangelical fervor gave energy to many of the charitable institutions, and many charitable organizations worked frankly to bring evangelical Christianity to the "lower orders." The British and Foreign Bible Society, Institution for Reading the Word of God in the Open Air, Religious Tract Society, and London City Mission anticipated the Salvation Army by several decades. Their approaches differed little from the Salvation Army, except in scope.

Churches themselves did very little before 1870 to relieve the poor of London. Indeed, the "respectable" classes owned the nonconformist sects; the nation (i.e., the elite and their deferential followers) owned the Established Church. None changed the working classes, which remained steadfastly indifferent about institutionalized Christianity. The dignity of St. Paul's Cathedral, the glory of Westminster Abbey, the elegance of all London's Anglican churches, and the proliferating but stoutly bourgeois nonconformist chapels made no real difference to the mass of working-class Londoners—or Englishmen, for that matter.

Yet more to the point of working-class difficulties than the religious societies were the medical charities of London. Twelve general medical hospitals, all charitable institutions, provided 3,700 beds in 1865. They could also manage to care for about 350,000 outpatients a year; special charities and dispensaries could provide for another 250,000 outpatients. Hospitals as the twentieth century knows them were, in fact, charitable institutions. The aristocracy and middle classes received medical services privately or in special elite establishments. Their doctors trained on the poor, much as they do today. St. Bartholomew's in Smithfield, St. Thomas's in Southwark (removed to Lambeth after 1866), the Middlesex in Marylebone, Guy's in Southwark, and the London in Whitechapel were famous teaching hospitals. St. Bartholomew's and Guy's had almost 600 beds each and were thus the largest. Of the other hospitals, University College Hospital and King's College Hospital indicated the trend of the future: the increased association of medical training with academic institutions.

Conditions, associations, and social status made a good many medical men radicals in the nineteenth century—in stark contrast to their twentieth-century counterparts. Harley Street still collected the very fashionable and wealthy doctors and of course continued to do so.

In general, the condition of the people took a turn for the better during the late 1860's. The Metropolitan Board of Works finished some of the major drainage systems. The nine water companies, now closely watched by the public, supplied purer water in larger quantities. All London authorities pressed the paving of streets, and new transportation facilities allowed some of the more prosperous workers to move out of the pestilential holes of the old areas, and to the newer suburbs. By 1870, improvers, reformers, and scientists had developed proper sewage disposal, adequate water supplies, and effective public health techniques to allow London's growth to speed up. Such improvements were minor influences, however, in the three-million-peopled city of Dickens' age.

The wealthier classes helped somewhat to improve conditions. But they most actively improved the conditions

nearest to them by a new technique, now used most frequently by the well-to-do under pressure from impinging
poorer classes: they moved. The sorting out of London's
social classes importantly affected the social attitudes of
future generations.

VI

Aspects of London, 1870

BY THE YEAR of Dickens' death new forces threatened destruction to the traditional diversity of London, and in its place promised to substitute an ever-shifting pattern of socio-economic class "quarters." London did not in the end lose its diversity, but it would be hard to exaggerate the impact of such changes that did occur. The aristocracy, the middle classes, and the working classes sought their own kind and no longer lived closely together as in the past. Until the nineteenth century, and actually for much of it as well, London had large areas which were made up of small "cells" of wealthy households (a square, or perhaps a street or two) near which shopkeepers and laborers lived in order to service and cater to the households.

A whole complex of factors changed these residential habits: the aristocratic desire to be as near as possible to the cultural and social center in the West End; the prosperity which expanded the aristocracy and drove up property values; the surge of the middle classes to "idyllic" suburbs; the railroad; and the unpleasant urban conditions where crowding, the port, and industry threatened health.

The aristocrats began the process in the late eighteenth century and early decades of the nineteenth cntury. They left the City and adjacent districts, moving to the squares and building estates of Bloomsbury, to some of the more accessible villages near London such as Clapham, to other segments of Bloomsbury, to Belgravia, and then to Kensington. Builders and developers constructed town houses for the wealthy, tailoring the Georgian plans to the demands of the new century. At first, the growth of aristocratic residential areas encouraged shopkeepers and artisans to stay nearby, in order to service the houses and establishments of the wealthy. But rapidly rising property values drove the less wealthy out of large sections of Bloomsbury and Kensington, for instance. Also, the West End encouraged the development of large-scale commercial establishments which catered to the wealthy. After 1850 the shopkeeper dealing with nonperishable, fancy goods had to compete without much success with such stores as Swan & Edgar (1812), Harrods (1849), and Liberty's (1875).

From their increasingly exclusive quarters, the aristocrats and would-be aristocrats could follow the proper schedule of their lives: politics, theater, the parks, the clubs, social events at nearby houses and at Court. Wealth alone did not create the schedule—but wealth in conjunction with "position."

The middle classes began to create their suburbs in the very early years of Victoria's reign. Such suburbs were, of course, satellites of London itself but still part of what Sir John Summerson called the "gross fabric" of the metropolis. Middle-class businessmen, clerks, and professionals traveled to the City each day, returning to their Gothic, Tudor, Romanesque, etc., "villas" at night. The villas, whether semidetached (duplex) or detached, gave to the *bourgeoisie* space and status. Naturally, the *bourgeoisie* were more anxious to separate themselves from the artisans or working classes, for the actual differences between the lower *bourgeoisie* and the upper working classes would be neither apparent nor real in the old city. When the middle-class family took a villa in a suburb, at least the differences became apparent.

The new bourgeois suburbs encouraged monotony and dreariness. No wonder their inhabitants wanted variety of architectural styles, for there could not be much distinction otherwise. Builders and developers carved up the estates of the "outer ring" (south, west, and north) for street after street of houses. Only shops, chapels, and churches varied the ripple upon ripple of housing. Important cultural institutions remained in the central portion of the city. Clearly, the inhabitants did not usually want the sort of variation which industry provided. When industry invaded one of the suburbs, the middle classes began to move elsewhere.

As never before, Londoners were identified according to class by the area in which they lived—or so the middle classes imagined. When the poorest clerks who could still be called "middle class" moved into a suburb, the wealthier *bourgeoisie* moved on. London and other British cities may have invented this dreary socio-economic game of musical chairs, but they allowed the American middle classes of a century later to perfect it.

The Victorian *bourgeoisie*, then, settled into living patterns very different from those of the aristocracy: head-of-family into the City at an early hour and home rather late (offices closed at six o'clock, usually); church or chapel; self-improvement activities; Sunday recreation; gardening. What we today call "commuting" weakened the proverbially tight-knit middle-class family, for the head of the household spent more time away.

One alternative living arrangement for the middle classes

in later decades has been the apartment or "flat." Apparently the first flats for the well-to-do were made available in the Victoria Station area in the 1860's.

Transportation developments made much of this nervous suburbanization possible in Dickens' lifetime. Bridges over the Thames gave South-Bank its great opportunity to expand explosively in the early and mid-Victorian decades. In the 1850's and 1860's the vestries and corporations paved more and more streets. Thousands of horse-drawn omnibuses seating many passengers and operated by several private companies connected portions of the metropolis. In Westminster, Holborn, and the City about 6,000 "cabs" served those who could afford them. But all of these vehicles made traffic slow and difficult. Peak hours at vital circles or crossroads must have been every bit as bad as today. Satirical cartoons about the confusion make the same points emphasized today.

Railways made the big difference for London. The national railway network which was constructed mainly in the 1840's and 1850's centered on London. All roads in the past may not have run to London, but all railroads did so. The ultimate extension of the railway system, certainly one of the major Victorian achievements, accentuated London's fabulous growth of the eighteenth and nineteenth centuries.

Within the metropolis railways allowed a rapid extension of suburbanization. Until the 1850's and 1860's the size of London's population staggered contemporary imaginations, yet most of the growth had logically filled in open spaces within a reasonable distance of Charing Cross (the commonly accepted center of the city). Railway development meant that suburbs could grow up several miles further out, and men could begin to see that all of southeastern England might well become London's immediate district. With the railways running efficiently out from relatively convenient stations both north and south of the river, middle-class Londoners discovered they could more easily travel miles into the city than short distances within the central area.

Railways of a different sort rescued central London, the national and suburban lines having compounded the original difficulties. On January 10, 1863, the first section of the "underground" opened for passengers. By 1866, the line connected Paddington Station with King's Cross, and its promoters soon pushed it on to Farringdon Square to the east. A new railway mania began in the metropolis with this new use for railways. Bunuel's Thames Tunnel, completed with great effort in 1825–43, could now be incorporated into a railway system instead of remaining a curiosity for tourists only. Fares dropped rapidly in the 1860's, and suddenly even workingmen could afford to live far from their regular employment. In the older middle-class suburbs to the west, many artisans and workingmen began to settle, pushing the *bourgeoisie* farther out.

Railways tied London's districts together, allowed London to absorb vast chunks of Middlesex, Surrey, Kent, and Essex, and bound the nation tightly to the metropolis. Few saw the ultimate consequences of all this expansion until the end of the century; Britain's leaders still puzzle over the ways to solve the massive problems.

Before 1870, railways also disrupted London's life—or, to be more precise, the construction of railways disrupted large areas. Since the first railway line had been opened in 1836 (to Greenwich), railway builders had wrecked thousands upon thousands of dwellings, largely working-class. We have seen what the impact was on St. Pancras, for instance. Even today city redevelopers plan sloppily, if at all, for populations forcefully shifted. In Victorian England, the displaced working classes crowded into old "rookeries" or poor districts. In the 1860's when underground railway construction relied chiefly upon the opencut, the railway builders displaced about 20,000 Londoners each year. Average annual construction of working-class housing did not keep up with regular population increase, little well with displacement. Working-class housing fell behind the actual need by at least 50,000 to 60,000 persons each year in the 1860's. Some writers thought it fell behind by a figure nearer 100,000 each year.

Other reconstruction also displaced thousands of Londoners: docks in the East End (especially St. Katherine's) and streets, for instance. Reconstruction in London did not compare with what Napoleon I and Napoleon III did to Paris, yet the various authorities executed some major projects. When added to the massive new building, the activity of the port, and the construction of railways, street reconstruction enhanced the impression of restlessness and perpetual change which London gave to Taine and other articulate visitors of the century. None of the reconstruction really changed the pattern of the city, for London still had no thoroughfares in 1870. Oxford Street at one and one-quarter miles remained the longest street in the whole metropolis. Other major routes might give some appearance of continuity, but changes of name and direction between districts always occurred. Such a pattern froze onto London's map the outlines of the old districts, whatever the railways might do.

Some of the major reconstruction is too exciting, and too vital to modern London, to pass over too quickly. Trafalgar Square, upon which construction began in 1826, replaced the previous, important conjunction of the Strand and Whitehall—in other words, major routes from Westminster and the City. John Nash planned the square, which was named "Trafalgar" in 1830. The north terrace up to the National Gallery was built in 1840; Nelson's Column was put up in 1839–42. As with so many London projects, Nash's scheme was a good deal grander than what actually resulted.

Nash also planned Regent Street and Regent's Park. The prince regent, later George IV, wanted a thoroughfare from Carlton House, his official residence on St. James's Park, to the new Regent's Park where he would have a magnificent country house. Much of the area in between the two points was chaotically packed with houses of the aristocracy and also with near-slums—all crammed together in the traditional patternless style of uncontrolled growth. Nash's plan was actually quite simple. The grand route would run northwest from Carlton House to Piccadilly, then by a graceful curve ("the Quadrant") on to the northwest until it crossed Oxford Street. It then would continue to Hanover Chapel, through Portland Place, and to the park. Park Crescent was brilliantly planned to open out the great street onto the park. In the park itself, the Regent intended to have his country house, allowing some other select houses as well. Surrounding the park would be carefully planned terraces of houses. Today, Nash's route is Carlton House Terrace, Waterloo Place, Lower Regent Street, Picadilly Circus, Regent Street, Oxford Circus,

Upper Regent Street, Portland Place, Park Crescent, and Regent's Park.

The Regent was flighty about most things, including houses. He tore down Carlton House in 1827, rendering the purpose of the scheme and its execution ridiculous. He never built the house in Regent's Park, turning to Buckingham Palace instead. One could hardly guess now that any grand plan existed at all, for Nash pieced together the whole route for very practical reasons. Also, the twentieth century destroyed much of Nash's construction. Still, the scheme resulted in a great open slash's being made in the old quarters. Parliament had granted money for the project in 1813 for this reason above all others. One can still admire the pieces of Nash's plan, but they no longer hang together visually or logically.

One major street project, New Oxford Street in Bloomsbury, was specifically intended to destroy perhaps the worst "rookery" in the metropolis, St. Giles', driving the inhabitants on to other such rookeries. Naturally, the planners did nothing to prevent further piling up of the poor and criminals elsewhere. New Oxford Street was built in 1845–47. It set the pattern for Shaftesbury Avenue and King's Way, both of which were later intended to replace particularly bad slums.

Dickens' contemporaries imposed a variety of organizational patterns on London. Besides the transportation network, we have previously looked at local government, the Metropolitan Police, parliamentary boroughs, and registration districts for vital statistics. One other, more familiar to all men than any of these, was the post-office districts: "E" for the East End, "EC" for the City, "WC" for Holborn, "W" for the West End and beyond, "N" and "NW" for the northern boroughs, "SW" for Kensington and beyond, "S" for South-Bank.

*   *   *

Dickens would not have enormous difficulty recognizing today's London as the direct successor of the "Great Metropolis" of the 1850's and 1860's. The great landmarks of the past remain; centralization has not totally destroyed district characteristics, though it has certainly qualified them. Administrators have solved the more obvious problems of Dickens' day, but the sheer weight of more than nine million people gives birth to new ones. Greater London with this vast population and certainly more coming grew out of the trends of 1850–70—that is, intense functional specialization, with all of its advantages and disadvantages.

Above all, Dickens would recognize the sophisticated, alert, tolerant vitality which was and is London.

Selected Bibliography

❦═══════❦

From among the hundreds upon hundreds of books and booklets on nineteenth-century London, I would note a few which might be of particular interest to the reader or are of such particular interest and usefulness as to be worth some extra effort to search out.

One can approach modern London (that is, London from the Great Fire of 1666 right up to our contemporary metropolis) through the most recent edition of *The Penguin Guide to London*. The guide is readily available, easy to use, and full of useful and reliable information about London past and present. For the reader or potential visitor whose interest deepens, Nicholas Pevsner's two marvelous volumes on London in his *The Buildings of England* are superb guides to the physical details of the city. Both are available paper-bound or cloth-bound. One volume is on *The Cities of London and Westminster* (1957) and the other on *London Except the Cities of London and Westminster* (1952). Pevsner's books are not easy to use as quick references, but they are worth every moment of time one would wish to devote to them. The great scholar of architecture is very likely to turn a casual interest in buildings into a veritable addiction. Another sort of excellent general introduction to the city is R. Clayton (general editor), *The Geography of Greater London* (1964). It has a very good bibliography.

Steen Muller Rasmussen's *London: The Unique City* projects one immediately into the very soul of London, as indeed does Ford Madox Hueffner's (Ford's) nostalgic little book called, in fact, *The Soul of London* (1905). Asa Briggs' *Victorian Cities* (1963) is an ingenious book with a good Chapter VII on London (though it is essentially on London after 1880).

Several works of interest fit together a sort of history of London, or collect all kinds of facts and sketches about the city. G. L. Gomme's *London in the Reign of Victoria, 1837–1897* (1897) was produced for the Queen's Diamond Jubilee. J. Grant's *The Great Metropolis* (2 vols., 1837), Charles Knight's edited *London* (6 vols., 1841–44) and also his *Cyclopedia of London* (1851) all provide much of interest. J. Hollingshead in *Ragged London in 1861* (1861) takes one on a tour of the "rookeries." H. J. Dyos, on the other hand, studies the middle-class suburb of Camberwell in *Victorian Suburb* (1954).

For London's economy, three books are good introductions: P. G. Hall, *The Industries of London Since 1861* (1961); James Bird, *The Geography of the Port of London* (1957); and T. C. Barker and Michael Robbins, *History of London Transport*: Vol. I, *The Nineteenth Century* (1963). Both Hall and Bird are concise studies in the Hutchinson University Library series. Other works are Sir John Clapham, *The Bank of England: A History 1694–1914* (2 vols., 1944); S. W. Dowling, *The Exchanges of London* (1929); and Walter Bagehot, *Lombard Street* (1871).

Nothing can quite compare to Henry Mayhew's *London Labour and London Poor* (4 vols., 1861–62) as an introduction to Londoners who lived in Dickens' London. Dickens must have thought so, too; he borrowed heavily from Mayhew. I know of no work such fun to browse in: the facts about characters, the illustrations, the feeling one has of really getting to know people. Mayhew's volumes are hard to find, but Peter Quennell has produced three volumes drawn from Mayhew: *Mayhew's London* (1949), *London's Underworld* (1950), and *Mayhew's Characters* (1951).

On Dickens and his work, a few of the many excellent studies would be especially useful. Edgar Johnson, *Charles Dickens: His Triumph and Tragedy* (2 vols., 1962), is a superb, absolutely essential biography. The University of Oklahoma Press has published a revised edition of E. Wagenknecht's excellent *The Man Charles Dickens* (1966). The same press has also published an English translation of Sylvère Monod's *Dickens Romancier*, under the title *Dickens the Novelist*. A book which I very much appreciate is K. J. Fielding, *Charles Dickens: A Critical Introduction* (2d ed., 1965). Other valuable works are K. Tillotson, *Novels of the Eighteen-Forties* (1954) (the chapter on "Dombey and Son"); J. H. Miller, *Charles Dickens and the World of His Novels* (1948); P. A. W. Collins, *Dickens and Crime* (1962) and also *Dickens and Education* (1963); and G. K. Chesterton's *Charles Dickens* (1906) and *Appreciations and Criticisms of Charles Dickens* (1911).

And, best of all, there is Dickens himself: *Bleak House, Dombey and Son, Oliver Twist, Our Mutual Friend, Great Expectations, Little Dorrit, David Copperfield, Martin Chuzzlewit, Pickwick Papers*, and much more!!

Index

Index

Index